design & make
non-precious
jewellery

Super Freak Zebra, Felieke van der Leest, brooch, 2007. Textiles. Photo: Eddo Hartman.

design & make
non-precious jewellery

KATHIE MURPHY

For Walter

WITH THANKS TO, Susan my commissioning editor and Sophie my editor for their patience, Macer, Eleanor, Christine and Walter for all their assistance. To all the contributors for their images and invaluable information and to those who gave up their time and expertise; Lorraine Gibby, Jonathan Swan, Michael Carpenter, Roger Taylor, Penny Warren, Sarah Packington, Annette O'Sullivan, Michael O'Brien, Jenny Llewellyn, Paula Hope, Sarah Graveson, Katie Hagley, Craig at Middlesex, Rachel Brockhurst at the Crafts Council, the Electrum Gallery, Dazzle Exhibitions, Lesley Craze Gallery, also my local library, the Brighton Art College library and the Workshop library, Lorna and David for their support and Linda Lambert for asking me to do this book.

DISCLAIMER

Everything written in this book is to the best of my knowledge and every effort has been made to ensure accuracy and safety but neither author nor publisher can be held responsible for any resulting injury, damage or loss to either persons or property. Any further information which will assist in updating of any future editions would be gratefully received. Read through all the information in each chapter before commencing work. Follow all health and safety guidelines and where necessary obtain health and safety information from the suppliers. Health and safety information can also be found on the internet about certain products.

First published in Great Britain 2009
A&C Black Publishers
36 Soho Square
London W1D 3QY
www.acblack.com

ISBN 978-0-7136-8729-3

Copyright © 2009 Kathie Murphy

CIP catalogue records for this book are available
from the British Library and the U.S. Library of Congress.

Book design: Sally Fullam and Sutchinda Thompson
Cover design: Sutchinda Thompson
Commissioning editor: Susan James
Managing editor: Sophie Page
Copy editor: Julian Beecroft
Proof reader: Jo Waters

Printed and bound in China

Every effort has been made to ensure that all of the information in this book is accurate. Due to differing conditions, tools, materials and individual skills, the publisher cannot be responsible for any injuries, losses and other damages that may result from the use of the information in this book.

Contents

1. how to use this book

While you are slowly taking your time to read and digest the information in this book, you should be keeping a **visual diary**. It is essential for artists and makers do this: it helps you to understand and observe the things you like and dislike, both of which are important in helping you to find your own method or voice for making jewellery. The images you tear out of magazines and newspapers (not books, please), as well as your drawings, photographs and note-takings, all feed back eventually at some point into your work. It may not always be apparent or immediate. The information does not all have to be kept in the same place. I have a wall of images I stick up in front of both my jewellery bench and work desk. I keep an ideas book, too, for jewellery shapes and fittings. The strangest things can become part of your work. I finally noticed how metal hooks and rings were cemented into the harbour side one holiday – simple, neat and clean – and this made me realise how I could attach fittings to my resin earrings! It seems obvious now.

This book will assume that the user has some knowledge of working with jewellery techniques and a basic workshop and toolbox. Many of the materials and processes do not require machinery (although it is useful), and much can be achieved without it. The old cliché of necessity is the mother of invention holds true. Where specific equipment is required, I have written this down under **What you will need**. It may be that for the purposes of trying things out you are able to find a particular tool or machine second-hand, or borrow it from someone else. Many techniques in jewellery become an area of particular expertise, and jewellers will often get another maker with specific skills to help in some way with the production of a piece. Thus it may be the case with some of the techniques in this book that someone else could do it for you. It is better that they do it really well than you do it badly. However, knowing what is involved will help you with the particular design or brief you have been given. I firmly believe that learning new skills is part of moving ideas and designs on, not churning out the same old pieces but wanting to push the limits of a material and try out new techniques and ideas.

When you have read about the material and its techniques, there are **suggestions** and **creative ideas** throughout and at the end of each chapter to help you get started in that material. **Work quickly and freely** to begin with, and don't worry about making a finished piece. You are now building up experience and information, which again will feed back in to your designs. **Keep notes** – you will be amazed how soon you forget how something came about. Also, learn to control the results of your test pieces. If you try out a particular technique again, do you get the same result? To help this handbook act as a reference manual as you work, I have set out simple subheadings under each material where possible, for instance, **Cutting and piercing, Joining and fixing, Forming, Colouring,** and **Finishes**.

Information and inspiration from drawings, photographs and notes for keeping a visual diary. Photo: William Teakle.

After you have tried your hand at a particular material, and feel comfortable with how it can be used, you can try out some of the projects at the back of the book to help you bring the information and your own ideas together to design and make a piece of jewellery using non-precious materials.

There is also an extensive list of suppliers, because finding small quantities of these materials is half the battle. Check their minimum order and carriage charge before you buy. If you have enjoyed trying out a certain material, A&C Black have further handbooks relating to more specific techniques, which will help you improve your knowledge and understanding.

Remember to work safely and not to affect or annoy others around you. Some of the methods are hazardous and odorous. Wear protective clothing and masks at all times when handling these materials, and store them safely. Most suppliers have a technical advisor, so be sure to ask them about the safe handling and use of any potentially hazardous material.

100 Test pieces, Tom Machin, 2006. Made with materials from one British woodland. Photo: Malcolm Hunt.

NON-PRECIOUS JEWELLERY

IMMATERIAL MATERIAL?

"Knowing there is nothing new in the world is the beginning of a good artist."
W. B. Yeats

In the last 20 years, what is now called studio jewellery, especially non-precious jewellery, has seen a huge increase in the types of materials and techniques used by makers. Many of these materials have been around for a long time though until now used in other areas of craft or life, and others have been revisited after a period of being out of fashion.

Non-precious materials have been used from the time people first made a hole in a shell or wove feathers to be worn as decoration or as a talisman; evidence of such practices are thought to be 90,000 years old. Materials like iron and plastic were used in the past in costume jewellery to mimic expensive precious jewellery, but more often ended up having their own distinctive character. Even today the weight of sentimental and personal associations can lend a piece of jewellery greater worth for its wearer/owner than can be measured by its sale value.

Finding your own voice without treading on the toes of other makers can seem daunting. I find using non-precious materials allows me to express myself a little more easily.

European jewellers tend to embrace a variety of materials, with the idea being paramount, whereas many British jewellers tend to have focused their work on one particular material. Everyone uses non-precious materials creatively. The adventure of discovering what a material is capable of and how you can transform it can take years rather than weeks. However, do not be put off, as you can still make something that pleases you, even if it isn't cutting edge, in a matter of weeks. Making by hand is time-consuming, and in our increasingly homogenised world something a little less commonplace can be and should be valuable. Above all, though, no matter what material you use, the quality of design, the execution of ideas and the craftsmanship should all combine to make jewellery of the highest standard you can achieve.

Bangle, Adam Paxon, 2005. Laminated, thermoformed, hand-carved acrylic. Photo: Paul Ambtman.

2. rubber

The two types of rubber shown in this chapter are silicone and latex. These are available as raw materials with which you can colour or cast, or which you can lay up as a skin to produce jewellery pieces. It is possible to buy readymade rubber pieces, usually industrial in nature, which are generally used as findings in a design. For example, rubber O-rings, tubing and cord are available in a variety of rubbers – nitrile, silicone, neoprene, polyurethane and fluorocarbon – but not generally available in many colours.

Silicone rubber is a flexible polymer, scientifically known as polydimethylsiloxane. The rubber has excellent resistance to extreme temperatures, and its tensile strength, elongation and tear strength are much better than other rubbers. A highly inert material, it fails to react with most chemicals, and as a result is more likely to age well.

Latex can be a natural or synthetic product. Natural latex is tapped from the rubber tree, *Hevea Brasiliensis*. As a natural material it will biodegrade completely. Ultraviolet light can cause latex to degrade, and contact with copper and its alloys should also be avoided. Some people have an allergy to latex, caused by proteins in the rubber. In this regard, latex from a different plant, the guayule, which produces a hypoallergenic rubber, is now being developed.

The term RTV means room-temperature vulcanising, which means it will set or cure without needing to be heated to a certain temperature. Check when buying, as some rubbers do require heating in order to set.

When using rubber in a design, consider the weaknesses of the material, namely that it may not have a high tear strength and that it may not be easily joined to another material.

Earconch, Kathy Vones, 2006. Silicone and silver.
Photo: John K. McGregor.

WHAT YOU WILL NEED

- ▶ mixing pots
- ▶ electronic scales
- ▶ a spatula
- ▶ protective gloves
- ▶ a scalpel or scissors
- ▶ plastic pipettes
- ▶ scrap acrylic sheet and materials to make masters or formers

TIP

Mix a small quantity at a time, as the pot life may not be very long.

FORMING

Silicone rubber is available in a number of types, either opaque or clear. Each manufacturer will have their instructions on how to mix the rubber, so do remember to read them. Generally, silicone is a two-part rubber that is measured out by weight, and the two parts are mixed to a certain ratio. Do not measure it by eye as this may result in an improper mix, with the rubber not setting properly. Even where you have measured properly, make absolutely sure that you mix thoroughly, as any base rubber that has not fully mingled with the catalyst will not set, leaving you with sticky patches. Once you have measured out the rubber you will have about 15 minutes of 'pot time' before it starts to set and becomes unpourable.

Liquid latex is set by air-drying it over a master shape or in a mould. The master shape may need to be dipped several times to build a sufficient number of layers. Each layer must dry before the shape can be redipped. Both rubbers can be thickened. With silicone this allows a more vertical skin to be applied without it dripping, and for latex it allows a faster build-up of layers.

Mixing silicone to paint over formers or pour into moulds. Photo: William Teakle.

CASTING

Both rubbers are used as the mould for casting into, but this does not stop them also being used as the casting material. Silicone rubber will need a sprayed layer of wax release agent to stop it from sticking to itself. It can be cast into a latex mould (see the chapter on resin for mould-making). It may be necessary in some cases to use a vacuum machine to get rid of all air bubbles.

CREATIVE IDEA

Using a sheet of acrylic, burr into it to create a pattern or texture, then carefully pour or paint the rubber onto the surface and leave to set.

COLOURING/DYEING

Silicone rubber can be coloured using special pastes and powders; pigments for polyurethane, acrylic paint or specific pigments such as UV reactive or fluorescent (see the **list of suppliers** at the end of the book). When using clear silicone you can add a little colour to keep the rubber translucent. Colourants for latex are also available, though note that the colour will dry darker.

TIP

Using readymade rubber tubing and sheet, add texture or colour. Paint directly onto the surface or fill up a tube with coloured rubber. Slice this up afterwards and lay discs down flat beside each other. Build a low wall around them and fill in the gaps with another pouring of rubber.

Painting and dipping masters in latex, which has had thickener added and left to air dry. Photo: William Teakle.

CREATIVE IDEA

Pin out some cloth or muslin. Pour rubber in a line onto the material and squeeze it through the fabric. Then leave to set to create a rubberised material.

CREATIVE IDEAS

Pour layers of different colours over a period of time, then cut and rearrange the rubber to form patterns.

Fold and stitch or glue pieces to make a 3D form. Stick using a contrast-coloured rubber.

Paint the rubber over different formers and shapes. Will it turn inside out, picking up the texture of what is underneath? Dip a shape into rubber and then leave it to drip carefully so that it dries but still looks liquid.

Try and incorporate another material or object into the rubber. As the rubber won't stick to it, think about how you can trap the other material or object.

CUTTING AND PIERCING

After the rubber has set it is best to cut it using a very sharp tool, whether scalpel or scissors. Rubber is not easily drilled, so any hole needed should be incorporated into the casting or lay-up. It is possible to drill some of the bought industrial rubbers with a dental burr or drill bit, but make sure the burr or drill is at its sharpest, or the rubber will tend to tear.

JOINING AND FIXING

Silicone rubber will only adhere to itself, which brings advantages but also difficulties too. When designing a piece you can consider these qualities – silicone's inherent elasticity and softness – as a feature of the work.

Latex can be stuck to itself with a solvent-based rubber-solution adhesive. This can cause the latex to curl up, but it also forms a good water-resistant bond. Alternatively, you can use a latex adhesive such as Copydex, though this will not be watertight. **Whichever you choose, make sure you work in a well-ventilated area.** These adhesives are available in hardware shops. Different types of glue can make latex deteriorate.

Other methods of joining and fixing these materials in place would be to hold under tension, to rivet using plastic, wood or metal, to sew, or to staple in place.

FINISHES

Neither silicone nor latex can be filed or polished. The desired finish on your work has to be thought about before you start, as the rubber will pick up the detail of whatever surface it comes into contact with. This characteristic can be used to great affect when creating a piece: consider, for example, a wood or corrugated texture, and a shiny or matt finish.

Neckpiece, Jenny Llewellyn, 2007. Silicone, phosphorescent pigment,
light-gathering polycarbonate. Photo: Jenny Llewellyn.

the gallery

	2	
1	3	4

1 **Cufflinks**, Katie Clarke, 1996. Silicone elastic. Photo: Patrick Gorman.

2 **Ring**, Andrea Halmschlager, 2002. Latex and Swarovski stones. Photo: Ulrike Halmschlager.

3 **Nigredo Brooch**, Elisabeth Holder, 2004. Gold-plated steel, latex, magnet and silver. Photo: Eib Eibelhäuser.

4 **Necklace**, Andrea Halmschlager, 2002. Latex and Swarovski stones. Photo: Ulrike Halmschlager.

3. plastics

In this chapter, five varieties of plastics are demonstrated: acrylic, resin, polypropylene, cellulose acetate and nylon. Each material has its own quite distinct working characteristics. Some of the plastics are more readily available than others. It is also possible to get cheap offcuts of a few of them left over from industrial waste, too small for their intended commercial use but a good size for jewellery. Plastic used in making jewellery has been around since the 1920s. Mainly associated early on with cheap costume jewellery, it has become a popular material with studio jewellers.

There are two types of plastic: thermoplastic, which can be heated and formed and will then revert back to its original shape if heated again, and thermosetting plastic, which undergoes a single change through heat and sometimes pressure to form a solid.

1   **Double-pebble earrings**,
    Wendy-Sarah Pacey, 2007. Acrylic and foil.
    Photo: Jeremy Johns.
2   **Sunburst neckpiece**, Nuala Jamison, 2006.
    Acrylic. Photo: Peter Mackertich.
3   **Snappy**, Karen Gilbert, 2007. Found plastic
    materials. Photo: K.L. Gilbert.
4   **Iris Flowers**, brooches, Iris de la Torre, 2007.
    Acrylic and rubber. Photo: Iris de la Torre.

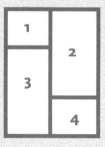

acrylic

WHAT YOU WILL NEED

- a piercing saw with coarse blades
- a band saw
- hand files
- eye protection
- an electric oven/hotplate
- clamps
- protective gloves
- formers (a mandrel, a glass jar, a wooden mould)
- stainless steel bowl

TIP

Keep the protective film on the acrylic while working with it for as long as you can.

MATERIALS

Acrylic or polymethylmethacrylate (PMMA) is a thermoplastic. It is available in clear sheet, rod and tubing forms, with a wide variety of coloured, transparent and opaque sheet, but a limited coloured supply of tubing and rod. Some of the colours available are light-emitting, and a mirrored acrylic sheet is also obtainable. It is also possible to dye acrylic. There are specialist places selling domes or dish shapes in acrylic, and also precision acrylic balls. Acrylic comes in two types: cast, which is more expensive, and extruded.

CUTTING AND PIERCING

Remember that it is essential to wear goggles and a dust mask.

Acrylic can be cut using a piercing saw (or a band saw for larger cuts) or by a specialist laser cutter. It is a brittle material, and care has to be taken when working with it as the material's swarf melts from the heat of the cutting tool. The swarf then cools on contact with the air and hardens into a solid, trapping the cutting tool so that it is almost impossible to get out. To ensure that this does not happen, take the cutting slowly, let the cutting blade dictate the speed and withdraw it frequently to keep it cool.

If you are cutting thin stock, run the blade at a fast speed and for thicker stock, at a slower cutting speed.

When cutting curves, take it slowly and work to the outside of the cutting line. For small curves and intricate shapes, the acrylic can be cut on a jigsaw.

For certain designs and production work, it is possible to get acrylic laser-cut. This produces very accurate cutting and the edge has an almost polished finish to it, although the laser does leave a very fine trace line. To drill acrylic, again work slowly as it is all too easy to get a drill bit permanently stuck in the plastic. If there is no protective film on the plastic, cover the area to be drilled with a piece of masking tape and mark the centre of the hole.

WHEN USING A BAND SAW, MAKE SURE YOU WEAR GOGGLES AS BITS MAY FLY OFF. IF NECESSARY, USE A WOODEN PUSHER STICK TO FINISH THE CUT, AND NEVER TRY TO PICK UP STRAY BITS WHILE THE BLADE IS STILL RUNNING.

Place the piece to be drilled onto a wooden block; this avoids the acrylic shattering around the hole as the drill bit comes out the other side. Secure the piece to the drill table in a small vice, jig or clamp, so that should the drill bit get stuck, the plastic won't whip around and cut your hands. Make sure you're continually lifting the drill bit up and out, allowing the swarf to come off and the drill bit to cool down. You can use a little oil or paraffin to help lubricate the drill and to cool it slightly. If a drill bit does get stuck, it may result in a ruined piece of work.

JOINING AND FIXING

Acrylic can be joined using glue. Only a few glues will work, so testing is necessary should you try out a different type of glue to any of those mentioned here.

There is a specific adhesive for acrylic called Tensol cement, of which there are two forms, one specifically for outdoor use. Suggested glues to try are cyanoacrylate, or Superglue (but do take extra care when using this, as it will bond skin), as well as Plasweld and Araldite or other epoxy adhesives. To achieve a good adhesion, make sure the surfaces to be joined are clean and have a keyed finish. Do not use too much glue, and make sure to clean up any excess around a joint before it sets. To weld acrylic use Plasweld or dichloromethane, a solvent which 'melts' the surface of the plastic to allow the material to bond and set. Use this extremely carefully as it is volatile.

Acrylic can also be joined through pinning, hinging, riveting or laminating. Sheet acrylic can be joined in layers, or laminated, through heat and pressure. It is usually best to laminate your piece before heating to form it.

First you will have to remove the protective film and ensure it is clean and grease-free. **Always work in a well ventilated area.** Heat the plastic uniformly in the oven to near 200°C (392°F). The material will soften in a short number of minutes so keep an eye on it; if you overheat the acrylic, it will bubble. Working quickly, as it will cool rapidly, remove the sheet from the oven onto a clean, flat, metal surface. Press the sheets together, either manually or by placing an even weight over the top, or by clamping them in place, or by applying even pressure using a press. Then leave the sheets in place until they cool.

Laminating a small area of a piece is also achievable. Heat the area over a hotplate or with a hot-air gun (see image on page 22).

Above: Drilling plastic using a pendant drill. Photo: William Teakle.

Left: Cutting sheet plastic; remember to wear safety specs. Photo: William Teakle.

FORMING (see image below and page 34)
Basic shaping can be achieved using coarse files, a linisher and burrs on a pendant drill. Always file in one direction. The file cuts as you push across the material, producing a lot of dust, so use a mask.

Acrylic is a thermoplastic, meaning that when heat and pressure are applied, it is possible to bend and shape the sheet, rod or tube. Should you not be pleased with the result, you can reheat and start again. To heat the acrylic use a small electric oven, one not also used for food. Remember to preheat your oven to 180°C (356°F), and keep checking the plastic until it is flexible. A former or mould is needed to shape the plastic; it should be something that can withstand high temperatures. **Always wear protective gloves when handling the hot plastic.** Depending on your design, it may be necessary to finish your edges using wet & dry papers and/or polish before heating and bending the acrylic.

For curved bends, use a mandrel or glass jar, and hold the plastic in place with even pressure and tension until it has cooled. For a straight-line bend, a wire heater and bender is best, though it can also be achieved without having to buy a special machine. If you haven't got one of these, you can try heating the piece locally along the area to be bent, using a piece of metal or wood to push against to give an even bend. To avoid a curved edge the line to be bent will need to be scored slightly. This can be achieved using a triangular file to file a shallow line.

To form a 3D shape use a female-shaped former and push the sheet in evenly, or, if using a male former, hold the plastic in place over it until it cools; alternatively, use both. This process can be done more easily for large pieces using a vacuum former.

COLOURING/DYEING

Acrylic is available in a wide variety of colours, but it is also possible to dye it. However, it only dyes on the surface of the material and not all the way through, so it can also wear off. Think about this when designing a piece using acrylic.

First and most importantly, wear gloves and work in a well-ventilated area. Over a hotplate, heat water in a stainless-steel bowl, and add a small amount of detergent to the dye bath to stop any scum from creating an unevenly dyed surface. To achieve the best colour, use Dispersol dyes. Add a small quantity of the powder to the dye bath and stir well to ensure it is completely dissolved. To assist the dye taking to the plastic a wetting agent can be added; ask the dye supplier for the best one to use. Tie a piece of nylon line or metal wire to your work and place in the dye bath, agitate and keep checking the piece.

Heat-bending plastic using a hot-air gun, see also the section on Cellulose Acetate for another method. Photo: William Teakle.

Dyeing acrylic and nylon showing colour variance achieved through length of time and overdyeing. For further information see section on Nylon. Photo: William Teakle.

Lobe Gardening, Sarah Crawford, 2003. Acrylic and formica. Photo: Richard Stroud.

FINISHES

The surface of acrylic can scratch easily, so take care while working on your piece. To remove any marks or to finish off, start with wet & dry paper and work up through the grades, from P180 (coarsest) through P240, p400 and P600 to P1000 (finest). Use the papers with plenty of water to keep the dust down. Lay flat sheets on a large, flat, smooth, waterproof surface; for curved surfaces wrap the wet & dry paper around a stick. Once you have finished off at P1000, rinse and dry the work.

To polish the work without a polishing motor, you can use a liquid or cream metal polish with a soft cloth and a lot of elbow grease. Otherwise use a calico or swansdown polishing mop with Vonax (a polishing compound for plastics) or stainless-steel polish. Keep the mop for this use alone.

TIP

It may be quicker and more efficient to heat a small piece of work using a hot-air gun than heating an oven for one tiny item.

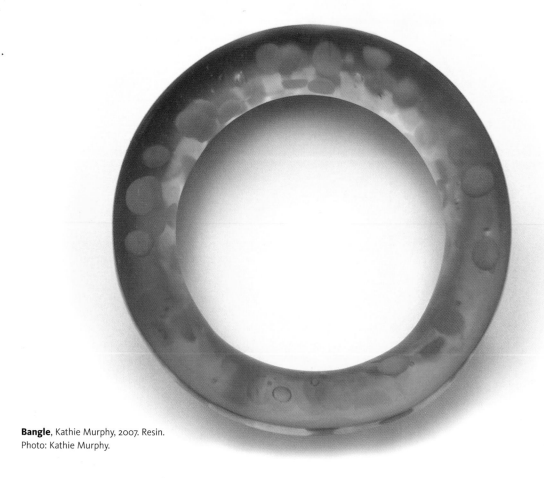

Bangle, Kathie Murphy, 2007. Resin.
Photo: Kathie Murphy.

SUGGESTIONS AND IDEAS

- If you overwork the acrylic, the material will produce stress cracks. Even so, see how far you can push the material while still maintaining control over it.
- Using sheet acrylic, cut a series of test pieces and on each one, by drilling and burring, try different textures. These could be filled with resin or overdyed. Once the colour has settled in the recess, remove the dyed surface colour using wet & dry. Alternatively, insert acrylic rod into the drilled holes; or heat the test pieces and hammer the plastic while it is soft; or heat the test pieces and then pass them between sheets of metal through the rolling mills to change their thickness or to transfer an embossed pattern from the surface of the metal.
- Laminate layers either through heat and pressure or by gluing. Then cut and rearrange the layers to form a new pattern or texture. Laminate clear acrylic through heat and pressure with different materials trapped inside.
- Make simple shapes from wood or firm casting silicone rubber, and form heated sheet acrylic over them.
- Try heating rod and tubing and bending them in different ways: curving, tight spiral bends, twists and coils, pulling into distorted shapes. Does placing silicone rubber cord inside a tube (which can be pulled out later) and gently curving it ensure that the tube does not deform?
- Start with a flat sheet and cut a pattern which, when heated locally, can be bent up to form a 3D shape.
- Try as many different joining methods as you can think of: end to end, right-angle joints, insertion joints, making a hole in a flat sheet and then curving acrylic rod through the hole.
- Think of ways to attach thin metal wire and other findings.

resin

WHAT YOU WILL NEED

▶ vinyl sheeting to protect your work surface

▶ good ventilation

▶ an organic vapour mask

▶ vinyl gloves

▶ electronic scales

▶ measuring cups

▶ lollipop sticks

▶ resin colour pastes

▶ cardboard and thin hardboard

▶ a hot-glue gun and sticks

▶ rubber moulds to cast into

TIP

Always allow in plenty of fresh air to clear the fumes, as any extraction for resin fumes, which are heavier than air, should be near floor level.

MATERIALS

Resins are a thermosetting plastic, which means that they undergo a single irreversible change to become a solid. They start as a liquid plastic and by the addition of a catalyst or hardener produce a chemical, exothermic reaction, which generates its own heat, to set the plastic solid. There are many varieties of resin, designed by industry for specific job applications. The most accessible resins for jewellery-sized casting are either polyester or epoxy resin. Polyester resin is available as a clear thin liquid that is translucent for colouring, or as a thixotropic or gel-like paste for lay-ups on vertical surfaces. The latter will pretty much always set with a tacky surface, as it is designed to be built up in layers and you need a sticky layer for the next layer to adhere to.

Epoxy resin is available in clear casting liquid and is translucent for colouring. Epoxy is very good for cold enamelling as it dries tack-free. It can be more reactive to moisture and heat than the polyester and thus may need very specific storage. There is also a non-toxic resin available, called bio-resin, but this can only be cast successfully with the use of a vacuum machine.

FORMING

Resin needs to be transformed from liquid to solid, and in this regard each resin will have its own specific instructions on how it should be mixed. Following these carefully is essential to your work setting properly and not catching alight. **Resin is highly flammable.** If it overheats during the course of the reaction, stresses and cracks can form within the material, which may then catch fire. The amount of catalyst or hardener specified by the manufacturer has been worked out so as to set the resin fully at a controlled rate. **Increasing the amount of catalyst does not successfully speed up the setting time.**

WHEN WORKING WITH RESIN, ALWAYS WEAR AN ORGANIC VAPOUR MASK AND PROTECTIVE GLOVES, AND ALWAYS FOLLOW THE MANUFACTURER'S INSTRUCTIONS.

Polyester resin is most easily measured out by volume in a calibrated cup. You should only use a catalyst dispenser, which will allow for drops to come out. For small jewellery castings, for every 100 ml (3.4 US fl. oz) of resin add 60 drops of catalyst; for larger castings, where the amount of resin used in one go is over 100 ml (3.4 US fl. oz), reduce the amount of catalyst to 30–45 drops.

TIP

Some clothes' wash liquids come with a millilitre-calibrated wash ball in polypropylene, which can be used to measure resin. Once the waste has set, you can crack out the old resin and reuse it.

Mould making using silicone rubber. When pouring silicone rubber into a silicone mould always use a spray wax release first or it won't come out. Photo: William Teakle.

TIP

Use an ice-cube tray to make quick, small colour and texture samples. A flexible one is best.

Resin will eventually set by itself without the use of a catalyst. Its shelf life is given as six months, although if stored correctly, it will last longer. So initially you should buy a 1 kg (2 lb 3 oz) quantity of resin. Once the catalyst has been added to the resin, depending on the room temperature, you will have a working time, or pot life, of around 15 minutes before the resin starts to become too viscous to pour.

Epoxy resin is usually measured out at a ratio of, say, 2 parts of A to 1 part of B, though again you should always follow the manufacturer's specific instructions. With epoxy you will also have a working time, or pot life, of around 15 minutes before the resin turns too viscous to pour.

CASTING AND COLOURING
Mould-making for casting

As resin is a liquid, it needs a mould to cast a shape. To make a simple open mould you can use a re-meltable PVC, or Vinamould or Gelflex, or latex or silicone rubber. Start by making a master shape in a heat-resistant material such as wood, plastic, Milliput or clay. Stick the master to a board using double-sided tape or glue. Using cardboard, build a wall around the master and hot-glue this in place. Heat the Gelflex or mix the silicone rubber, though take care with the Gelflex, as this melts at 180°C (356°F). Pour it into the box containing the master. Leave to set for about 24 hours. If you are using latex, dip the master shape, building up layers, then peel the skin mould off the master. Depending on the master shape, this type of mould may need support from a plaster surround so as to prevent the resin from distorting it. Once the mould is ready, it can be used for repeated castings.

Necklace, Sarah King, 2005. Bio-resin.
Photo: Jeremy Johns.

TIP

Cast up slowly in many layers of colour. Vary from clear to opaque. Let each layer almost set before pouring the next layer.

CREATIVE IDEAS

Using a balsawood shape, paint layers of resin over it like an enamel.

Try different ways of applying fittings to the resin.

Create textured space within the resin by making a textured master: try pasta, rice or rubber cord in a repeated pattern over a shape.

Colouring

After you have added your catalyst or hardener, you can mix special colour pastes into the resin before pouring it into a mould. The amount of paste you can add is up to a maximum of 10% of the resin by volume. It needs to be completely mixed into the resin or it will not set. A surprisingly tiny amount of colour can go a long way, and the pastes can also be mixed to make a new colour. The colour can be controlled to allow a translucent colouring or they can be completely opaque. Once you have coloured the resin, it can be poured into the mould and left to set.

Colouring ideas you may like to experiment with:

- Mix a small amount of resin with one opaque colour paste and another amount of the same catalysed resin in a translucent colour. Next, add the opaque to the translucent, cautiously so that they don't mix, and carefully pull the colour about. The two colours form a pattern within the resin and set at the same time.
- Tip your mould at an angle to produce a gradation of colour within a layer of resin, and then, with the mould level, cast another layer.
- Try casting a piece with built-in recessed areas, which can then be filled in with another colour (or colours) of resin.

CUTTING AND PIERCING

Whether you are drilling or cutting, the resin will produce a lot of very fine dust, so it is important that you wear a mask. It is best to try and cast the resin into the final shape required so that there is as little work as possible to do to the resin afterwards. Where possible, avoid a lot of cutting. However, if the need does arise, resin can be cut using a piercing saw, band saw or jigsaw. Put a coarse blade in a piercing saw. With a band saw or jigsaw, take the cutting slowly, allowing the blade to dictate the speed at which you cut. The heat of the blade can make the resin burn and produce smelly fumes. Again, it is best if you can avoid drilling resin. It is possible, using resin-resistant rubber or plastic tubing, to make a hole in the casting. Make locating holes in the mould and place the tubing in, then pour the resin around and leave to set. Afterwards, remove the tubing and you have an instant hole. Where you do need to drill, take it slowly; you can use a drill bit or a dental burr and avoid the cutting edge chipping the edge of the hole. Repeatedly remove the drill bit to allow waste material to drop out of the hole and to let the drill cool down.

JOINING AND FIXING

The best way of joining resin to itself and other materials is to use it as an adhesive. However, it may need to be thickened to ensure that it does not seep over the rest of the work. Clean up any excess immediately. Where you are joining other materials to resin, such as metal, you can use an epoxy or Superglue. Finally, depending on the thickness of the resin, you may need to do a test first to see if it is too brittle to attach by pinning or riveting.

FINISHES

After the cast has been removed from the mould, it may still have a slightly sticky surface. This can be removed by filing it with a coarse file. Again, try to avoid filing large areas of resin and take account in your initial design of the need to file the piece once it is finished. **Always wear a dust mask.** File in one direction only. Then refine the surface further with wet & dry papers. Start with P240 and move on to P400 and then to P1000. Work wet as much as possible to keep the dust down. Once you have a smooth finish, the surface can be polished or left matt. On a matt finish, to bring out the colour rub the piece with baby oil and a soft cloth. Polish the resin on a polishing machine using Vonax compound.

CREATIVE IDEA

Add dry items to clear resin: sequins, buttons, leaves, foil, flowers, wire, sand or other resin shapes.

Red Rock Ring, Polly Wales, 2006. Resin and metal. Photo: Polly Wales.

polypropylene

WHAT YOU WILL NEED

- ▶ Stanley knife
- ▶ scalpel
- ▶ steel rule
- ▶ some masking tape
- ▶ cutting mat

TIP

Tape everything into position before making a cut. PP is slippery, and this prevents mistakes and potential loss of fingers.

TIP

Work out the scoring lines and planes to produce a variety of 3D shapes.

MATERIALS

Polypropylene (PP) is a thermoplastic, which has a variety of industrial uses, from packaging and textiles to car parts. It has a very high melting point and chemical resistance, is water-repellent and also very tough and flexible. Unlike other plastics, polypropylene has an extraordinary resistance to fatigue from flexing. It can also be machined and printed. These properties make it very versatile for all sorts of packaging. Polypropylene is also recyclable. Mainly available in a range of colourful sheets, it is possible to buy clear rod and PP tubing.

CUTTING AND PIERCING

Polypropylene can be cut with care using a strong craft knife and a steel rule. As the sheet tends to be available in a thickness less than 1.2 mm, it is easier to cut more accurately by hand. Use a cutting mat and make sure that it does not move around whilst you are using such a sharp blade.

Scoring and bending PP sheet using a steel rule and craft knife.
Photo: William Teakle.

Brooch, Gill Forsbrook, 2005,
Polypropylene. Photo: Gill Forsbrook.

CREATIVE IDEAS

Try screen-printing and other methods of mark-making on the PP.

Try as many different types of scored line and curve as you can think of; see what shapes and 3-D folds can be achieved.

Find different methods with different materials to hold a sheet curved into a tube shape in place.

Examples of methods of joining sheet plastic. Photo: William Teakle.

CREATIVE IDEAS

Can a texture be raised on the surface with an engraving tool or melted creatively with a heated tool?

Weave different colours of sheet together, and also with different materials such as paper or fabric. Once woven, how do you then keep all the ends in place?

PP can be drilled to make small holes, but where a larger, crisp, clean hole is required, it may be better to use a hand tool called a wad punch; this is a steel tool with a hollow circular cutter which works a bit like a hole punch in removing material. You can still use a larger drill bit, but you may find the edge is not as crisp or as easy to clean up. The swarf produced has a strong bond with the material and does not come off or clean off neatly.

FORMING, SCORING AND BENDING

As already described, polypropylene is a great material for producing a scored bend that does not become weakened in the process of bending or using it. Make the score line on the outside edge of the intended fold. Use a little less pressure than if you were going to cut through the sheet. To create a curved surface, the sheet can be easily bent to a curve with your hands as it is flexible and thin, but remember that it will revert back to a flat sheet shape if not held in position under tension. The following two processes are available to you for forming 3D shapes with this material.

Expanding Bracelets, Louise Miller, 2003.
Polypropylene. Photo: Full Focus.

JOINING AND FIXING

Polypropylene cannot be stuck together easily using glue and other methods of fixing, so joining it to itself or another material has to be considered carefully. Riveting, stapling, binding or pinning are all possibilities that can be used, as well as making splits or cuts in the material itself to hold a bent or scored sheet in position.

FINISHES

Without removing too much material, keep the edges as cleanly cut as possible to avoid having to trim up any mistakes. Wet & dry paper helps smooth the edges but should not be used on the surface of the piece. If you do use papers on the surface, it makes the plastic turn whitish. It cannot be polished.

CREATIVE IDEA

Create texture and colour by laminating different materials in between the PP, or find methods of capturing something in the plastic itself. Is it possible to score and bend it afterwards?

cellulose acetate

WHAT YOU WILL NEED

- heatproof gloves
- an oven or hotplate
- coarse files
- a vice or clamp
- formers or moulds
- rolling mills or a fly press

ALWAYS REMEMBER TO WEAR HEATPROOF GLOVES WHEN WORKING WITH HOT PLASTIC.

MATERIALS

Cellulose acetate (CA) is a thermoplastic. It is derived from the organic materials of wood and cotton and is one of the few plastics that comes from a renewable source. The wood or cotton is pulped to produce the cellulose, which is then mixed with acetate and colouring and, through a series of processes involving heat and pressure, formed into a sheet. It is available in a huge range of colours and patterns, though not easily available to buy.

Cellulose acetate is used in the manufacture of costume jewellery, spectacles and guitars amongst other things, as well as being the material the first Lego bricks were made of.

CUTTING AND PIERCING

Drill cellulose acetate with drills or burrs. Remember to keep removing your drill bit from the hole and clean away any swarf. CA leaves a very clean edge and does not go whitish in the cut area in the same way as other plastics. Even when burred, it does not mark or discolour significantly along the cut edge.

Cut using a piercing saw, band saw or jigsaw. Take it slowly to prevent any overheating. Swarf comes away easily from the cut and leaves a very clean edge (see images on page 21).

Heat-forming cellulose acetate and acrylic using male and female moulds and formers. See also the section on Acrylic for another method. Photo: William Teakle.

Twig and Leaf Necklaces,
Katy Hackney, 2006.
Silver, cellulose acetate.
Photo: Sussie Ahlberg.

TIP

Heat the sheet cellulose acetate and then try forming it around a mandrel or glass jar, over a male mould, then a female mould, and then with both male and female which may help to produce a more accurate and deeper draw, or distortion, of the material.

FORMING

As a thermoplastic, cellulose acetate can be heated and formed using some kind of pressure. Heat the material to around 100°C (212°F) (at which point it becomes flexible), then shape into a curve by bending it around a former, holding it in place until it has cooled. Apply an even pressure along the whole piece to prevent any buckling or unwanted distortion. It can also be shaped using a mould; press the warm shape into the female mould or shape over a male mould. The mould shapes can be made using wood, metal or any other firm heat-resistant material. The larger the piece to be heated, the more important it is to make sure the whole piece has heated up evenly (see images on page 22 and 34).

JOINING AND FIXING (see image on page 32)

As with other plastics, because you cannot solder, other methods have to be found to attach jewellery findings or other materials. Try riveting, pinning or linking the cellulose shape/s. Small joins can be made with Superglue where the plastic has been drilled or cut to allow an accurately sized piece of another material to be inserted.

Comet Bangles, Lesley Strickland, 2006. Cellulose acetate. Photo: Sarah Wills.

CREATIVE IDEAS

Laminate the sheets and build up a shape this way.

Roll the sheet through the rolling mill whilst still hot from the oven. Put the sheet in between two sheets of copper or brass. Will it emboss if you etch one of the sheets first? Also, consider trapping some copper wires in there too.

The thin cyanoacrylate will form a good bond where there is a larger surface area to adhere to. A form of weld can be achieved using acetone to 'melt' the surface of the cellulose so as to bond with itself. Work in a well-ventilated area and paint the acetone onto one surface of the piece, bearing in mind that it may be necessary to work into the surface a little. Take care, however, to work neatly and not to 'melt' any surface around the join that will show and cannot be cleaned up easily. Put the piece in a vice to ensure a strong join.

Slot Necklace, Lesley Strickland, 2006.
Cellulose acetate, silver.
Photo: Sarah Wills.

FINISHES

Coarse files can be used to file down the edges of the cellulose acetate. Remember to use different files for plastics than for other materials. The cellulose files easily and cleanly. After filing, wet & dry papers can be used to achieve a very smooth, warm surface finish. Work up through the grades from P400 to P1000.

A soft polish can be produced using Vonax, but make sure that the surface has been really well papered up to P1000, as otherwise every mark will show. Any shallow marks will not polish out in the same way as might be the case with other materials during this process.

nylon

WHAT YOU WILL NEED

▸ a stainless steel bowl
▸ a hotplate
▸ plastic retrievers
▸ protective gloves

TIPS

Use large drinks bottles to store used dye but make sure they are CLEARLY MARKED with the contents, and remove any old labels.

If you have a small lathe, try as many different ways as you can think of to create shapes with it.

MATERIALS

Nylon is a synthetic polymer, also known as a polyamide (PA). Natural polyamides are silk and wool. It is a hard, tough, elastic thermoplastic with strong wear and chemical resistance. There are two types of nylon suitable for jewellery use, nylon 6 and nylon 66, which come in sheet, tube and rod form. Nylon 6 (the number refers to the number of carbon atoms in the monomer) is cast and nylon 66 has a high mechanical strength and is suited to engineering purposes. Another readily available form of nylon is monofilament, which can be found in small quantities and a few different thicknesses in the form of fishing line at your local angling shop. You can also obtain precision balls in nylon, as well as a huge variety of nylon textiles.

Nylon has a melting temperature of 128.33°C (263°F) and will dissolve in phenol and formic acid. It will dye easily with Dispersol dyes and fairly well with Dylon dyes.

CUTTING AND PIERCING

Nylon sheet, if thin enough, can be cut with snips or a Stanley knife, or more easily on a band saw and less so with a piercing saw. Although it feels like it is cutting easily, swarf from nylon melts very quickly out of sight into a sticky mass that is difficult to remove and will trap the drill bit, making it immovable. To avoid this happening, you need take out the piece being cut very regularly, and remove any swarf. Be warned that swarf from nylon does not detach itself easily from the rest of the plastic in the same way as that of other materials such as cellulose acetate; be careful not to remove more than just the swarf.

Nylon can be drilled using drills and burrs, although its soapy quality can make it less easy to drill neatly. It is advisable again to constantly remove the drill bit and clean away any debris.

JOINING AND FIXING

As with many of the plastics, nylon cannot be soldered and does not easily glue. Alternative methods of joining nylon to itself and to other materials have to be tried out. Riveting, pinning and stapling are options. With sheet nylon it maybe possible to use cuts or shapes within the sheet and to interlock pieces, but this will depend on the design (see image on page 32).

Newsprint Neckpiece, Karen Whiterod, 1998. Nylon. Photo: Karen Whiterod.

FORMING

Sheet nylon can be formed simply by curving the piece by hand, but it has to be held in place under tension to keep the shape. Gently warming the nylon will allow you to shape it a little more easily, though overheating it can lead to it losing its springiness. It may well be necessary most of the time to have finished working on the sheet (including colouring it) before forming the shape.

Some shaping of nylon monofilament/thin rod can be achieved through drawing it down or rolling it through the mills, but again this can only be taken so far and would have to be worked out as you gain experience of the material. More certainly, nylon monofilament can be given shape through weaving and textile techniques without having a direct impact on the material itself. The elasticity of the nylon allows it to keep its shape well under tension.

Rods of nylon around 10mm (0.39 in.) or more can be turned on a lathe, the tooling being the same as for lathing aluminium. Again, due to its low melting point, it is important to work slowly.

CREATIVE IDEAS

Using a heated iron, apply texture to the surface by melting it and pulling the material.

Which works best: knitting or crocheting monofilament?

Using monofilament as a bristle, trap bunches of the fibre in nylon or another material.

FINISHES

Nylon cannot be easily filed, and any surface on a solid piece should be carefully finished on the lathe to a smooth finish. If the piece has been linished, use finer grades of belt sandpaper, making sure that no stray pieces of grit from the paper have embedded themselves in the nylon. Using wet & dry paper, working through all the grades from P240 to P1000 will result in a smooth surface. Gently rubbing the surface with pumice powder will produce a gentle matt finish. Before dyeing any work, you should finish the piece to the required surface quality.

COLOURING AND DYEING

Nylon takes surface colour well to a reasonable depth, though it will not dye all the way through on pieces of a thickness of 4 mm (about 0.15 in.) or more. **First and most importantly, wear gloves and make sure the area is well ventilated.** Heat water in a stainless steel bowl to just under boiling point, add Dispersol dye to the water (about 1 teaspoon to a litre (2 pt 3 fl. oz) of water), or use a tin of Dylon dye. **Whichever you use, make sure the container is clearly marked with the contents.** Make sure the powder is completely dissolved or it will leave streak marks on the work. Add a drop of detergent to stop any scum forming which could leave an unevenly dyed surface. A wetting agent can be used to help the dye penetrate the plastic, thus securing a greater depth of colour. Ask the dye powder's supplier about which one to use. The strength of the solution and the time the piece is left submerged in the dye bath will depend on the strength of colour you want. You can keep dipping the piece in and out of the solution. To help find the work in the dye bath, make an S-shaped hook and sit this over the edge of the bowl or tin, then tie monofilament to your piece with a loop at the end to put over the hook. It is possible to reuse the dye solution until it becomes exhausted (see image on page 22).

SUGGESTIONS AND IDEAS

- Experiment with dyeing different types of nylon stock. Keep a note of the time it takes to achieve a certain colour. Try overdyeing one colour on top of another colour.
- Try printing on the surface or, using a steam iron, transferring a photocopy to sheet nylon. Place another piece of paper between the iron and your work to stop it melting. What other materials will act as a stop-out on the surface: PVA glue, masking tape, other kinds of tape or wax?
- Using different lengths of nylon tubing, stop-out the outer surface. Dye one colour inside, then apply different textures to the outer surface using a heated tool or engraver, before dyeing again in a different colour. You could plug the ends of the tube to stop the new colour affecting the first colour, or not, as you see fit.

TIP

Start with the four basic dye colours – red, blue, yellow and black – and mix them to create your own colours.

Oscar Wilde Quote Neckpiece, Karen Whiterod, 1998. Nylon. Photo: Karen Whiterod.

the gallery

1	2	
3		4

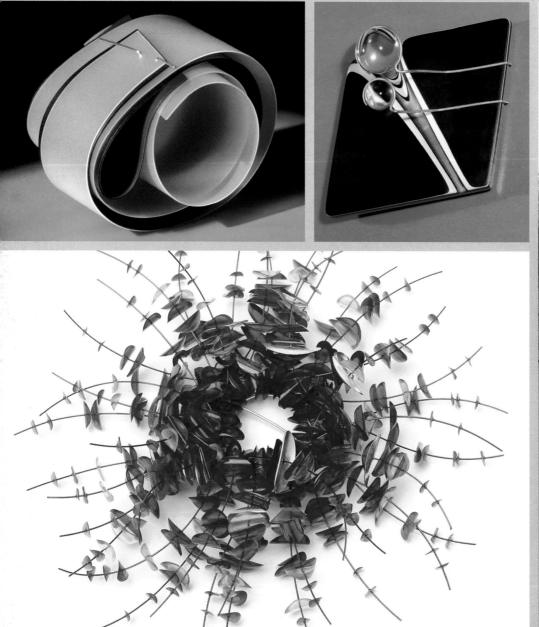

1 **Bangle**, Gill Forsbrook, 2005. Polypropylene. Photo: Gill
   Forsbrook.

2 **Batman Brooch**, Caroline Smith, 2006. Laminated plastic and
   acrylic. Photo: Mick D'Elia.

3 **Sporadic Brooch**, Alena Asenbryl, 2007, various plastics.
   Photo: Anthony Crook.

4 **Kandinsky Circles Neckpiece**, Nora Fok, 2007. Nylon
   monofilament. Photo: Frank Hills.

the gallery

4. wood

Wood is not a commonly used material in jewellery but it is certainly one we are used to in many aspects of our lives. As there are so many different types of wood, this chapter will leave that choice to the maker, but it is certainly worth trying ideas and tests in as many different sorts as possible to make it easier to choose the right kind of wood for a particular piece of jewellery.

There are two categories of wood: hardwoods and softwoods. The terms can be misleading as they do not necessarily refer to a wood's material hardness. Hardwoods tend to be the wood of deciduous trees, with a finer, more continuous grain, and the softwoods those of conifers, which are more porous. Wood is used in furniture, flooring, building and in certain musical instruments, to name just a few uses; so it is also available in a number of forms, including solid block pieces and thin veneer sheets, plywoods and cork. Some woods, also known as exotic woods, are naturally more patterned in their grain. Some are colourful, including pinks and oranges as well as near-black, while others are very pale and blonde.

After a tree is cut down, the wood needs to be seasoned before it becomes workable, meaning that the moisture in the cut wood needs to dry out to prevent warping or splitting. Knots in wood are the point at which a branch grew. They can either be a problem, where the grain of the knot is denser than the rest of the material, or they can leave a beautiful pattern in the wood.

Petal Necklace, Nutre Arayavanish, 2007.
Wood laminate. Photo: Suthipong J.

WHAT YOU WILL NEED

- burrs
- saws
- wood glue
- sandpapers
- wire wool
- beeswax
- a scalpel
- a cutting mat
- offcuts of wood
- coarse files

TIP

When working with wood, remember to wear a dust mask and to properly extract the dust.

CUTTING AND PIERCING

For jewellery purposes, try to obtain smaller pieces of wood where possible so that you are able to cut it without large specialised machinery. If this isn't possible then your local timber merchants may do it for you. Use a band saw or jigsaw to cut larger pieces to a workable size. Depending on what you are trying to make, you may then find it is better to remove material with a belt sander or linisher. To avoid the wood becoming weakened or stressed, cut along the grain, and to avoid burn marks on the cut surface, take the cutting slowly as the friction and heat of the blade can cause it to blacken. Cut smaller, thinner wood with a piercing saw used with a coarser saw blade, size 2 or 4. With experience you will find what suits both the particular type of wood and your own ease of working.

For cutting veneers, use a scalpel or a Stanley knife. If you are doing long or intricate cuts, you may need to tape the work down to stop it moving.

Drill wood using a pillar drill or, on smaller work, a pendant drill. When drilling a large hole, start with a small-sized drill and work up. For cutting larger holes, it may be possible on certain pieces to use a flat drill bit or a circular cutter. Burrs can be used to carve the wood or apply decoration.

FORMING

Creating a 3D shape with wood on a scale appropriate for jewellery is a process of either removing material or building it up (for instance 'laminating' in the 'Joining and fixing' section). Starting with a solid block of wood, your piece can be cut then filed with files or rifflers, or the waste material can be removed more quickly by linishing to the required shape or lathing it using handheld cutting tools. When removing material from a natural product, you may find hidden faults within the piece you are working on. Keep a close eye on your work as you go, constantly checking the process. Looking carefully at a piece of wood will help you decide if it is the right piece for the job, a judgement that becomes easier with experience.

It is possible to bend pieces of wood, either by kerf-cut bending or by steam bending, both processes that are more effective on thinner pieces of wood. Kerf-cut bending entails removing sections of wood as a series of slots along the inside edge to be curved. These should be cut to a depth of no more than two thirds of the thickness of the piece, so as to avoid splitting. Glue can be put in the slots to hold the curve in place. The slotted section can be veneered either side to hide the cuts in the wood.

Steam bending is more complicated but works by the heat from the steam dissolving the bonds between the fibres in the wood, allowing it to curve without splitting or cracking; once the piece has cooled those bonds are re-formed. The steamed wood is placed in a mould or jig of the desired form, clamped in place, and left to cool and dry. Methods for steam bending can be found on the internet, including steaming small pieces of wood wrapped in a wet cloth in a microwave.

JOINING AND FIXING

Wood can be built up into a form quite easily by laminating pieces together. Make sure the surfaces to be joined are smooth and clean; in addition, make sure that they touch in all places or you will get pockets of glue. Use a PVA wood glue which dries clear, or other brand-name adhesives such as Cascamite; this is a powdered resin glue to which you add water, which when dry, forms a waterproof bond. To ensure an even pressure, clamp the pieces between newspaper or polythene and flat solid sheets of wood or some other material.

TIP

Another method of creating a curve is to build up glued layers of veneer clamped between two formers, a male and female cut to the required curve, and left until dry.

CREATIVE IDEAS

Using as many different types of wood as you have available to you, try to create as many different degrees of curved surface as possible, using different thicknesses, either by linishing or kerf-cutting.

Wood and cork test pieces showing piercing, burring, laminating and kerf-cut bending. Photo: William Teakle.

CREATIVE IDEAS

Laminate contrasting woods together and create pattern by cross-cutting and laminating together again. Laminate circles of wood to create tubing or a hollow shape, thus dispensing with the need to drill or lathe out a solid piece.

Find twigs and fallen wood from hedgerows, leave to dry, and cut and shape test pieces.

Using only flat pieces or dowling, find different methods of fixing these in place to create a 3D shape. They may need to slot into something or be sewn together.

Make the wood look as if it is a soft material.

Try laminating and carving cork.

Smaller-scale methods of joining used by furniture-makers could be a method for fixing pieces of wood, such as bridle or mortise and tenon joints.

An alternative to gluing pieces together would be to rivet or pin one piece of wood to another using wooden dowling or metal rod or tube. Take care, however, that the pressure from the pin or rivet is not such that it will split the wood.

Metal findings can be attached with an epoxy or Superglue. Make sure that the hole or slot made in the wood is exactly the right fit for the metal piece, and roughen the surfaces to increase the bond.

FINISHES

Once the piece is formed, remove file or making marks using different grades of sandpaper from coarse to fine.

Wood can be dyed to produce an artificial colour, and being a porous material it will absorb any dyes down to a good depth below the surface. There are wood stains which allow the grain to show through and there are also bleaches to lighten the wood's natural colour. Procion dyes also work to produce bright colours in the wood.

Decoration can be applied to the surface of the wood either by marquetry, which is a technique of building up a picture or patterned surface using thin veneers of wood in different colours cut and fitted together, or by pyrography, which uses heated tools to burn a pattern or picture into the surface of the wood.

The next stage is to use wire wool and beeswax to further polish the surface. To seal the wood, it can be varnished or a coat of shellac can be applied. There are many varieties of varnish and surface finish, which may or may not suit your purposes.

Brushstrokes Neckpiece, Hayley Mardon, 2007.
Dyed, laminated plywood, and gold leaf. Photo: John K. McGregor.

the gallery

<table>
<tr><td>1</td><td>3</td><td rowspan="2">5</td></tr>
<tr><td>2</td><td>4</td></tr>
</table>

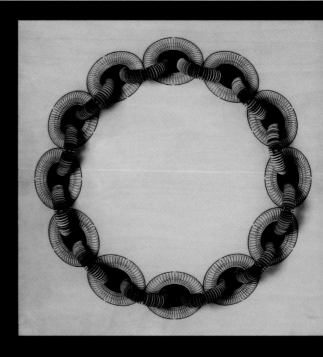

1 **Tree Rings**, Amy Watson, 2007. Ebony, rosewood. Photo: Brian Fischbacher.

2 **Antfarm Brooch**, Hayley Mardon, 2007. Dyed wood and beads. Photo: Michael Morton.

3 **Petal Necklace (detail)**, Nutre Arayavanish, 2007. Wood laminate. Photo: Suthipong J.

4 **Brooch**, John Field, 1991. Cocobolo, African blackwood, boxwood, bone, metals. Photo: J. Field.

5 **Three Brooches**, Katy Hackney, 2006. Plywood, Formica, bamboo and other materials. Photo: Sussie Ahlberg.

5. paper & leather

Paper and leather share certain characteristics, having similar material properties and sharing techniques with which to form and pattern the surface. One place where leather and paper can come together is in the form of a book. Early materials used for making marks on for man to document and communicate with others include stone, clay, bark, cloth, papyrus and parchment. Evidence of the earliest forms of papermaking come from China around 100AD and it is said that papermaking was inspired by observing wasps build their nests. The knowledge slowly spread westwards with varying techniques and processes becoming more mechanised. In contrast, leather processes appear to have developed around the world simultaneously, with a number of methods for preparing or tanning the hides. Both materials have been used to make a vast range of objects used by humans, they can both be made to be hardwearing and stiff as well as soft, pliable and colourful by dyeing. Leather has been used over time for containers, clothing, accessories and coverings, and paper in various forms has been used to make such vastly different things as furniture, packaging, armour, carnival floats and stage scenery.

Neckpiece, Kayo Saito, 2005.
Polyester paper, pearls.
Photo: Kayo Saito.

paper

WHAT YOU WILL NEED

▸ a cutting mat
▸ a scalpel
▸ a wad punch
▸ a steel rule
▸ a bone or bamboo folder
▸ an awl
▸ a food blender
▸ a washing-up bowl
▸ some newspaper
▸ some new kitchen cloths

TIP

Cover your work surface with polythene sheeting: it's wet work. Plastic pots and lids make quick and simple formers or moulds. A deckle can be used over a mould to give the paper neater edges; it is a frame the same size as the mould but without the screening.

Using the RT stamping system to cut out repeated shapes in paper with a steel or acrylic tool. Use a vice or fly press to apply the cutting force. Photo: William Teakle.

MATERIALS

Paper we are used to handling everyday, from letters and money to newspapers, is quite a different thing to that of handmade paper. Paper is made by breaking down the hydrogen bonds in a material such as wood, cotton, linen, hemp or rice. The separated fibres are amalgamated to form paper and left to dry in the air. It is quite possible to make paper by recycling materials such as used paper, cotton clothing and more recently, a welsh company has made paper using sheep droppings! Paper is characterised by its weight, usually in grammes, and by size, such as A4. Handmade papers are much sought after by artists and bookbinders and are available in a huge selection of colours and textures. Making your own paper is fairly simple, whether making sheet form or a papier-maché where it is combined with glue to create a more solid 3D shape.

CUTTING AND PIERCING

For a clean and accurate cut, use a very sharp scalpel or some form of rotating cutter; cutting with scissors is less precise. A wad punch or single-hole-punch tool can be bought to make neat small holes. To

Armpiece, Angela O'Kelly, 2005. Paper, elastic. Photo: Angela O'Kelly.

make a continuous line of holes, you may find a leatherworker's rotating hole punch will do, depending on the type of paper, or else use a template with pre-registered holes through which you can pierce with a needle or drill. A steel drill can be used on thicker paper. A template in a thin wood or card can be made for cutting around where repeated shapes are needed. It is also possible to make your own shaped cutter, a bit like a pair of scissors, from stock steel using an RT stamping system (see glossary).

FORMING

Construction of form and shape in paper is achieved by folding, bending, rolling and layering.

Origami (or papyroflexia) involves a complicated series of folds to produce a 3D paper form or raised pattern on the paper similar to a concertinaed effect.

The direction of the paper in relation to the crease is known either as a valley or a mountain fold, though it is also possible to achieve curved folds in paper. To make a fold, you first need to score the paper with an awl. Make sure the metal spike has a rounded end so that it doesn't cut or tear the paper. Also, work on a cutting mat to make sure the scored lines do not mark the surface of what you are working on. Where it is necessary to keep repeated folds evenly spaced, mark out the pattern of lines to be scored in pencil; once the

TIPS

The internet has many sites devoted to origami with downloadable instructions for making a huge range of shapes.

Try scoring and bending as many patterns as you can think up using lines and curves; don't worry if they are not successful.

awl has made the scored line, the pencil line can be removed with a clean art eraser. An aid to making smooth creases and burnishing is a tool called a 'bone folder', resembling a slightly thicker, rounded and gently curved lollipop stick; as with any tool, this can be shaped for specific purposes. After creasing the paper, carefully bend and push the paper in a logical fashion in the direction of the required fold.

Papier-mâché is the process of layering paper strips that have been moistened in a water-based glue, such as wallpaper paste or PVA, on top of each other over a former. The layered strips are then left to dry into a strong hollow object. Other fine materials can be trapped within the layers to create texture, or once dried the finished object can be painted and decorated.

Paper can be laminated with an adhesive, and under pressure, into a solid block that can then be turned on the lathe.

Another method of forming and shaping paper would be to do it whilst making your own paper. The damp paper is laid over a mould shape and left to dry slowly. Alternatively, an acetate shape is placed on the mould and a paper sheet is made as usual; once this has been couched and has dried out a little, it will come away from the acetate in that shape. This too could then be carefully shaped over a mould. A nearly dry sheet can be pressed in between a sandwich of two wooden outer panels and with newspapers or felt next to an etched or textured metal plate, foamcore cut-out, cardboard, fabric or linocut to emboss the paper, leaving a raised surface. Generally, the thicker the paper, the deeper the raised area will be.

To make your own paper, you will need a mould, which is a frame over which a fine material screening has been stretched. You'll also need a pile of folded newspapers or towels that fit into a tray with sides, which is then covered with a kitchen cloth and wetted with water. Called a 'couching mound', this pile helps ease the damp sheet of paper off the frame or mould. A new kitchen cloth is needed in between each sheet as it is laid on the mound, so have a pile ready to hand. For the pulp mixture, torn-up bits of old paper (not newspaper) can be used or combined with shop-bought cotton or abaca pulp.

Place the paper and pulp into a washing-up bowl and cover with warm water. Transfer this

TIP

Colour can be added when making your own paper by using coloured papers such as tissue paper into the pulp, or by adding natural or chemical dyes.

Forming paper using papier-mâché over plastic formers, or using acetate when making hand made paper to create a shape. Photo: William Teakle.

Brooch, Nan Nan Lui, 2007. Paper, metal,
Photo: Nan Nan Lui.

Brooches, Naoko Yoshizawa, 2004. Washi paper, thread.
Photo: Naoko Yoshizawa.

mixture to an old blender (though only fill it halfway up) or use a handheld blender. Blend for 15 seconds, at the end of which the mixture should have a very thin porridge-like appearance and should feel very smooth. Make sure there are no lumps. Agitate the pulp in the washing-up bowl if it has settled, then in one continuous swift movement lower the frame into the mixture at an angle on the far side of the bowl, and lift it towards you until it is horizontal. Jiggle it gently just below the surface to make the pulp fibres settle evenly, then lift up and allow the water to drain through. To release the paper onto the couching mound, hold it long side nearest to you and turn the mould over so the paper is facing the cloth. Press it down, applying even pressure as you bring it down onto the mound. When you have a pile of paper sheets in between cloths, place them in a sandwich of newspaper with wooden boards

East is East, Mahta Rezvani, 2005.
Second-hand book, leather.
Photo: Mahta Rezvani.

TIP

Will your own made paper score and bend? Can you set findings into it?

either side and press out the water, either with a press or by standing on it for a few minutes. Hang the individual cloth with the paper on it to dry. The cloth can be carefully peeled away from the sheet of paper when it has dried.

JOINING AND FIXING

Paper can be glued. Make a few tests with different glues to find the best one for your purpose as there are many types of glue suitable for paper. Other methods of joining could include stitching or binding it with threads, using a needle or making holes with a punch or, pinning it in layers to a sheet of metal using a rivet or tubing which has been soldered in place to the metal. Also, test adhesives for joining paper to other materials such as metal, fabric or plastic; for certain designs, you may need to back the paper or reinforce it.

FINISHING

Bought papers have a variety of surface finishes, shiny, matt or textured. To keep the finish intact, make sure the design is suitable and work cleanly and carefully. To protect the surface of some papers, you may need to use a varnish or if you are making your own paper, add starch or size to the pulp to make the surface less porous.

leather

Leather makes an ideal material for jewellery in that it is warm, supple and tactile, and available in many colours and textures. It can be used in many similar ways to paper. When it is cut, it does not need finishing, other than maybe by dyeing the edge a different colour. There are tools for engraving the leather and for punching holes or shapes, and others for paring down the thickness and scoring in order to make a crisp crease in the material. After it has been dampened with warm water, leather can be shaped or embossed either by hand or over a mould with a little gentle heat. However, the only leather this works with is undyed or vegetable-tanned leather. Being supple, it folds easily without creasing, but to keep thin leather stiff may mean backing it in some way. One piece of leather can be joined to another by being glued with appropriate adhesives such as PVA, and/or it can be stitched. A special tool is available for making a series of evenly spaced holes for stitching. As with paper, leather can be laminated.

TIP

Using a simple pattern of cut lines in the paper or leather, explore different methods of twisting the material back on itself through the cut or split. With paper, run the edge of a scissor blade along the paper between your thumb and index finger, to make it curl.

Cuff, Lucy Godfrey, 2006. Etched leather.
Photo: Ann-Marie Ramkissoon.

the gallery

1	2	
3		4

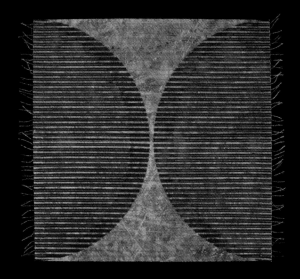

1 **Implements**, Magie Hollingworth, 2008. Recycled pulped paper and fibre. Photo: Mike Simmons.

2 **Rope Bangle**, Fiona Wright, 2007. Recycled Financial Times newspaper. Photo: Simon Armitt.

3 **Separation II**, Helyne Jennings, 1988. Photo: Helyne Jennings.

4 **Necklace**, Polly Glass, 2007. Lasercut leather. Photo: Polly Glass.

6. textiles

Textiles can be made from many different materials. The first textiles can be dated to tens of thousands of years ago, and evolved from threads, yarns and cords. Evidence exists of 3-ply and 2-ply cord made from flax and hemp and even nettles, with various treatments involving heat, water and drying being used in their manufacture. Palm leaves, bark and grasses were used as they were, untreated. Twisting the cord increased its strength, and by knotting it, prehistoric man used the cord to produce a flexible structure like a net or bag. Another prehistoric method that did not involve spinning or weaving was felting. The wool fleece fibres worked together to make a thick matted material that was amazingly waterproof, windproof and warm.

Textiles have developed significantly over thousands of years into the kinds of woven fabrics we wear today; from using dyed threads to produce a pattern, to printing onto the surface and modern 'intelligent' fabrics. Nowadays, textiles can be technologically highly advanced, but the original techniques are still applied too, whether natural or synthetic fibres are being used. A jeweller's concern is to use methods that will turn the material into a wearable object – techniques such as embroidery, felting, knitting, crochet, weaving and braiding. You could also make your own thread or cord from scratch, or dye your own colours; and it need not be expensive if you can find a way of using up remnants and scraps. In this chapter, each heading is a particular type of textile, and rather than itemise as individual subheadings all the different jewellery methods, each one outlines the basics for that material.

1 **Bracelet**, Tanvi Kant, 2006.
Recycled silk sari. Photo: Tanvi Kant.
2 **Tangerine**, Veronica Grassi, 2005.
Thread, soluble film, Velcro.
Photo: Sussie Ahlberg.
3 **Pin**, Naomi Seager, 2006. Felt,
steel, silver. Photo: Naomi Seager.
4 **Neckpiece**, Julie Hedges, 2006.
Linen. Photo: Julie Hedges.

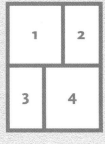

felt

WHAT YOU WILL NEED

- ▶ bubble wrap, rubber car mat or textured plastic mat
- ▶ hot water
- ▶ soap flakes or detergent
- ▶ felt-making needles
- ▶ a towel
- ▶ plastic containers (small for forming and large to hold the hot soapy water)
- ▶ a large block of upholstery foam

CREATIVE IDEAS

With dry-felting, work different colours into the surface or add other fibres such as silk.

Wet-felt in small areas onto another fabric such as silk chiffon.

MATERIALS

Wool fleece comes in as many varieties as sheep, each one having its own particular characteristics. Some are better than others for making felt, particularly if worn next to the body. Felt can be made using a wet or dry process. The fleece recommended for use by a beginner, and for jewellery, would be merino, which produces a smooth, fine felt. Merino is most suited to the wet process of making felt (see below). Wool fibres used in the dry process or in needle-felting need to be a little coarser – for instance, Romney. Synthetic fibres such as polyester batting can also be used in needle-felting.

Before it can be used to make felt, the wool fleece needs to be carded, meaning that the fleece has been cleaned and the fibres combed out into a batt or roving. A batt is a fluffy sheet of wool, and a roving is long organised lengths of the carded fibres. Along the length of the wool's fibre are little scales which open and close. By using hot water, the scales open, and the process of rubbing and agitating the wool tangles the fibres together. When the wool cools down, the fibres are held together firmly by the scales closing on each other. After the felting stage the next procedure of steaming, beating, rolling or needling the material, known as fulling, compacts and shrinks the fibres further.

DRY AND WET METHODS

DRY FELTING

Dry felting requires very little equipment. You will need a piece of firm foam and a selection of felting needles. These come in different gauges and shapes. Raised barbs along the sides of the needle cause the wool to felt, though watch out for their very sharp points.

The surface onto which you work is the piece of foam. Place small tufts of torn-off wool onto this surface, and starting with a 36-gauge triangular needle, stab or poke the needle repeatedly into the wool, working the material into the shape you want by rolling, folding and twisting it. The fibre will go exactly where it is poked: poking only near the surface of the wool will firm up the top layer while the inner ones stay squashy; while deep poking, where the needle goes in up to three quarters of its length, creates more solid shaping. Take the needle out of the work the same way it went in as

Bangles, Mandy Nash, 2007. Norwegian merino, Wensleydale, Shetland wool fleece. Photo: Mandy Nash.

Dry felting with foam and needles: shape the wool rovings and needle repeatedly or, using a blank of felt sheet cut to shape, build the felt surface using the needles and rovings. Photo: William Teakle.

TIP

Avoid patting the wool, as this does not achieve anything. Also don't roll the fibres back and forth when there is a central wire or former; roll in one direction. Rubber gloves with textured palms can protect your hands and also help agitate the fibres.

Using the wet felting process to shape a form using roving and a small plastic bottle, hot water, soap and bubble wrap to full. Photo: William Teakle.

TIP

With all the textile techniques it is possible to dye your own pieces and create your own shades and colours. Check with the dye supplier for the dye best suited to your particular type of fibre or cloth. You can use either natural or synthetic dyes.

the needles can break easily. Work at it until the piece is as firm as you want it to be. Then, using a finer needle (40-gauge), poke the surface of the felt in different directions to tighten it further. If the needle has left behind little holes, it is possible at this stage to wet-felt it, which will smooth over the fibres.

WET FELTING

For wet felting, first of all make sure you have a towel to hand as it is best to handle the roving with dry hands. Prepare the surface you intend to work on, whether bubble wrap or another flexible textured surface such as a bamboo sushi mat. The amount of wool you need will depend on the size of your finished work; but bear in mind that wool shrinks in the felting process by between a third and a half its original size, so you will need longer lengths to start. Have ready some hot soapy water. Gently pull off lengths of roving from the ball of wool and lay them evenly side by side on the mat in an east–west direction, so that they just overlap. The next layer should be laid in the opposite direction to the one below it, so north–south. Keep building layers, each time changing direction in this way. The thickness of the final piece will depend on the number of layers of wool.

Sprinkle hot soapy water over the wool and your own hands, and gently firm down over the piece to remove any air bubbles. Make sure that the wool is completely wet through, though not sodden; water should drain slowly away from the work, not make a puddle. Cover the wool with plastic and rub the surface in a small circular motion for three minutes, taking care that the wool layers do not move. Keep checking and

Necklaces, Anna Wales, 2007.
Felt, silver. Photo: Anna Wales.

add more hot soapy water when needed. Once the fibres have matted together enough for you to pick up the piece safely, it can be turned through 90° and the felting process continued. This procedure will ensure that the felt shrinks evenly from all sides.

Next, the piece needs to be 'fulled', which is the process of thickening the felt by moving the fibres together. To do this, roll up the work and tie firmly, once, in the centre, then roll it back and forth for five minutes or so. Unroll the work and roll it again in the opposite direction, applying slightly more pressure, for another five minutes. Repeat the unrolling and re-rolling until you are sure the work is completely felted; it will be up to half its original size and, as all the layers will be meshed together, should be impossible to pull apart. Rinse the work in cold running water and leave to dry.

50 meters Necklace, Keren Cornelius, 2006. Linen thread. Photo: Keren Cornelius.

SHAPING AND FORMING

Felt can be formed into a shape as you make it by using a former. You can use plastic pots or cardboard. Wrap the former or mould with between one and three layers of combed roving, and dunk it into a bowl of hot water, completely wetting the wool. Add a few drops of soap, and carefully work this in the direction of the wrapped roving. Keep the piece wet and continue to smooth the fibres together, working back in any pieces that come away from the surface. When the piece feels firm, increase the pressure by rolling or agitating it, still on the mould, on a work mat or surface. Alternatively, wrap the piece in bubble wrap, bubble side in, and use your fingers to work the felt surface. When you are happy with the quality of the outside surface, remove the piece from the former so that the inside can be felted by working the inner surface with your finger into the mat. If it shrinks too much, stretch it back over the former. Work it in this way until the piece is felted, then rinse and dry the felt.

As described in Dry felting previously, any shape can be made by pulling, twisting and rolling the wool into the shape you want during the felting process. Ball shapes are fairly easy ones to start with.

CREATIVE IDEA

Try making solid shapes in other textiles as well as felt. What hollow shapes can be made in felt? Felt over a copper wire allowing it to be bent and shaped. How do you stop the ends poking through?

fibre

WHAT YOU WILL NEED

- ▶ a crochet hook
- ▶ knitting needles
- ▶ various braid discs
- ▶ hot-and-cold-water-soluble fabric
- ▶ an embroiderer's frame

CREATIVE IDEA

Knit or crochet in copper wire or plastic-coated telephone wire.

MATERIALS

There are natural and synthetic fibres in all sorts of colours and thicknesses. For jewellery purposes, using the best quality you can find is imperative. Make sure it is the right type for the way you wish to use it – for example, some threads might jam up your sewing machine or might not be strong enough for the braiding. Consider also whether the thread will stand up to the rigours of being handled and worn. As discussed in the introduction to this chapter, threads, yarns and cords have existed for hundreds of thousands of years. Traditional jewellers tend mainly to use them for stringing, but an increasing number of studio jewellers employ them in making pieces using a particular technique. For the purposes of this book there are too many techniques to mention, so if you are interested in a particular method, follow it up yourself, either through one of the suppliers mentioned at the back of the book (most firms have a technical adviser) or by searching the internet. Fibres can be woven, crocheted, tatted, knotted, knitted, bound, braided or used in embroidery. Below are a few techniques you could try, with the idea in mind of creating a 3D shape. All the techniques use very little equipment.

With knitting and crocheting the form will come from flat pieces, which are then sewn together to create the shape, or by forming the

Examples of Kumihimo and French knitting. Photo: William Teakle.

Using embroidery on water soluble fabric. Photo: William Teakle.

Bat Girl Brooch, Felieke van der Leest, 2007. Textile, plastic toy, gold, cubic zircona. Photo: Eddo Hartmann.

Not Waving Necklace, Laila Smith, 2006. Hand- and machine-stitched textile. Photo: Laila Smith.

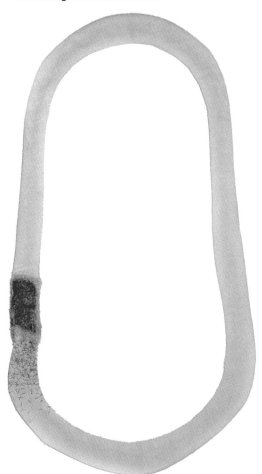

shape in the process by building on to a circle to create a tube that increases or decreases in diameter. The type of stitch used will also create a pattern.

A similar process would be that of **knotting**. The mechanics of knotting consist of the core, the material that runs continuously throughout the structure, and the binder, the flexible material that is knotted over the core. A simple method using half-hitch knots is enough to construct a three-dimensional shape. The shape is determined by the core over which the knotting is done, or by a former whose shape can easily be removed.

Braid-making is not so much a method by which you can create a 3D shape, but a much smaller-scale means of creating pattern and texture by plaiting threads. The braid can vary in cross-section from round to square to flat lengths depending on the technique used to make them.

Tablet-weaving is very simple and uses a simple flat weaving card. The warp yarn must be strong, as it takes all the tension and twisting, but lighter threads or yarns can be used for the weft. Lucet, or cord-making, a technique that dates from the Middle Ages, produces a square cord. The Japanese **kumihimo** craft of braiding can be made simply with a *hamanaka* disc; this technique

CREATIVE IDEA

Use different basket-weaving techniques on a smaller scale, with using paper, cloth, ribbons or barks.

Weight of the World Glove, Ann-Marie Ramkissoon, 2006. Leadcore line. Photo: Ann-Marie Ramkissoon.

is similar to the really simple method known as French knitting, except that in this case the threads are braided down the central hole as opposed to being 'knitted' or looped. The Japanese used these braids traditionally for kimono belts or on sword handles. More complicated techniques of kumihimo are used to make flat braid.

A special **embroidery** fabric can be used to make soft sculptural pieces of jewellery. The fabric can be embroidered by hand or machine and then dissolved in either hot or cold water, depending on the specific fabric used. The stitches, be they straight, circular or zigzag, must link up with each other. On cold-water-soluble fabric (CWSF) the stitches should not be concentrated in one section, as this weakens the fabric. Work evenly. For hot-water-soluble fabric (HWSF) the density of stitches depends on the type of work. Different shapes can be achieved but remember that the stitches must interlock. Any excess material can be torn off around the finished embroidery. With CWSF, the embroidery is placed in a bath of cold water and in a couple of minutes the fabric dissolves, or a damp brush can be used on any excess CWSF until it has disappeared. For HWSF it is advisable to use good-quality colourfast threads because the fabric is dissolved in a bath of water of 70–80°C for a couple of minutes. If a lower water temperature is used, the embroidered fabric will take longer to dissolve, but this does allow you to mould it into shape by removing it from the water before it is completely dissolved. The form will then hold its shape.

MATERIALS

From the fibre or thread comes the cloth. As with fibre, the available range of woven fabrics is enormous and need not be costly; the offcuts of dressmakers and upholsterers are typically the ideal size for making jewellery. Here, too, you should use the best possible fabrics, for the quality of the materials could affect the quality of your work.

Shaping the cloth to produce a 3D shape can be done using some of the following methods. Assembling a pattern of cut shapes, the material's seams can be allowed to show or be carefully and neatly hidden away. Overlock any seams where a frayable fabric has been used. Pattern cutting is a skill in itself and you would have to keep detailed notes along the way of each piece so that it could be repeated.

Shape can also be given to the cloth by stiffening it in some way whether through folding and creasing like origami, or using a fabric stiffening solution, or by joining or fixing it to a more solid form. Another method might be to stitch with an elastic thread, thus altering the shape of the cloth in a certain area. Using elastic with a smocking technique can create surface texture and pattern. A stretchy fabric could be formed over a core shape or along wire. The flat cloth can also be rolled and scrunched with different methods of stitching, binding, stiffening or holding the cloth so that it does not lose its shape.

CREATIVE IDEAS

Stitch layers of shaped cloth together to create form, or stitch together consecutive cloth shapes with a contrasting thread.

Work on devising various methods of incorporating a jewellery fitting into felt, fabric or cord.

Stitched Brooch, Lina Peterson, 2006.
Textile, dip-coated metal.
Photo: Lina Peterson.

the gallery

1 **Formation**, Jenny Bich van Lee, 2007. Silk organza, thread. Photo: Kathy Dickinson.

2 **Green necklace**, Sarah Keay, 2005. Enamelled wire, monofilament. Photo: Shannon Tofts.

3 **Chrysanthemum Neckpiece**, Masako Hamaguchi, 2003. Machine embroidery. Photo: Ulrike Halmschlager.

4 **Armadillo Hood,** Nora Fok, 2007. Nylon monofilament. Photo: Frank Hills.

7. metals

Trying an idea for a piece of jewellery in copper before proceeding to precious metals is a common practice, and a useful one for any novice jeweller. Other metals inexperienced jewellers may have used are brass, gilding metal and steel for tool-making; far less likely are aluminium, titanium and stainless steel. One of the delights of using plastics is the opportunity they bring to introduce colour into jewellery without resorting to precious stones or paint; but it is also possible to achieve colour with non-precious metals, through anodising, printing and patination.

For reasons of space, I have not been able to include every kind of metal in this chapter but have concentrated instead on those that are more familiar and more easily available. It is assumed that the basics of working in metal are already known; certain techniques are outlined in the chapter but the treatment is by no means comprehensive. However, if you aren't too familiar, there are enough tips to get you started in a particular material, and if you enjoy it, you can research further techniques in jewellery classes or other books.

1

1 **'Hang Luce' Badge**, Mike Abbott, 1991. Mixed metals, paint. Photo: Abbott and Ellwood.
2 **Rainbow Snake Necklace**, John Moore, 2006. Anodised aluminium. Photo: John Moore.
3 **Getting to know you,** animated brooch, Lindsey Mann, 2004. Printed, anodised aluminium, wood stand. Photo: Helen Gell.
4 **Cuffs**, Lorraine Gibby, 2007. Photo-screened, anodised aluminium. Photo: Steve Speller.
5 **Neckpiece**, David Poston, 1982. Hot-forged stainless steel. Photo: Phil Burton.

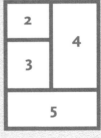

aluminium

WHAT YOU WILL NEED

- a hotplate
- 2 roasting dishes or disposable aluminium flat dishes
- some wax crayons
- some colour-permanent pens
- a foam eraser
- linocuts
- masking tape
- a pencil
- Copydex glue
- aluminium inks
- some aluminium dyes (powder)
- large liquid containers (approx. 2–3 litres)
- a roasting thermometer
- a palette

TIP

Keep your anodised sheet airtight and moisture-free with a silica gel sachet, and it can last up to six months, although the colours will tend to fade over time.

Applying different surface finishes to pre-anodised aluminium sheet using inks on a sponge, brush, stamp, lino cut and permanent pens, and with wax crayons and glue as a resist. Photo: William Teakle.

MATERIALS

Aluminium is the most abundant metal on the earth's surface. It is not found in its raw state, as the metal is too reactive and is found combined with other minerals, usually bauxite ore. The process whereby the metal could be easily isolated was not realised until the 1850s. Indeed, it was considered such a rare metal that Napoleon III is said to have had a dinner service made from it for special guests. More commonly associated with the aeronautical industry and domestic products today, its capacity for being anodised allows bright colours to be introduced to jewellery.

Aluminium is highly reactive and forms a fine oxide layer on contact with air. Anodising can render this changed top layer to a specific thickness, thus making the surface even more resistant to corrosion. The layer is formed of crystals that are initially porous, which allows the aluminium to be painted more easily or coloured by dyeing. The crystal layer can be sealed by boiling the metal in water, and in any case the moisture in the air will eventually bring about the same result.

Aluminium is a lightweight metal, malleable and non-magnetic. It can be cast or extruded and has a melting point of 660°C (1220°F). It is possible for you to anodise aluminium, but for the purposes of this book I have used pre-anodised sheet, which is available in a shiny or matt surface finish.

CUTTING AND PIERCING

Make sure you keep fingerprints off any pre-anodised sheet that has not been sealed. It is best to colour the sheet of aluminium first, then once it is sealed to cut and pierce afterwards. Cutting can be done with snips or a piercing saw, while piercing can be done using drill bits in a pillar drill or pendant motor. A flashing, or burr, does occur when drilling; lubricate when drilling and this will help reduce the size of the burr.

COLOURING

Work as cleanly as possible so that the aluminium sheet does not become marked. Remember that the surface is very porous and will absorb all grease and liquid. The sheet will dye on both sides, though the manufacturers do not guarantee that the back will colour as brightly. To work efficiently, it is best to work on a few sheets at a time, so have everything planned ahead – the colours, the patterns and what you will be using that sheet for. It is possible to create colour layers when dyeing the metal, an end result achieved in two stages.

TIP

Annealing the aluminium with a gentle flame can revive the undyed anodised layer by driving out moisture.

CREATIVE IDEA

Before trying to dye a whole sheet, cut up the pre-anodised metal sheet into test pieces. Make a note of the techniques and colours used to obtain a certain effect.

Dyeing final overall colour to inked aluminium sheet at 40°–50°C. It can be overdyed to create another colour or gradation of colour. Do not boil or it will seal the surface. Photo: William Teakle.

Stage one is using inks, either water-based or solvent-based, or permanent-ink pens. The ink dyes for aluminium are very expensive but, as very little is needed because the colour is so intense, they will last a long time. However, there are only six colours.

Oil-based printing inks are another, more affordable alternative. Have a palette so that you can mix colours, or spread the ink out for use with a printing roller. Areas can be stopped out with PVA or Copydex (these rub off when dry), wax crayons or non-porous tape. No colour will take to these areas, which can be dyed in stage two or left as pale silvery aluminium. It is possible to use printing techniques, and in this regard a simple method is to transfer toner photocopies onto the surface by ironing, the toner acting as a stop-out that can be removed after the metal has been coloured with inks. Rubber stamps you make yourself, or linocuts, can also be used with the inks. The process can be very painterly or very graphic at this point. Allow the inks to dry thoroughly before proceeding to stage two.

While the ink is drying, you can get ready either a water bath for sealing the surface if your sheet is finished, or a dye bath if you are planning to overdye a final overall colour. Clever control of colour can be achieved by overdyeing one colour on another to produce a third. If you have used inks, these will not be affected. Cold-water Dylon dyes can be used up to 50°C (122°F), but not hot dyes as these will seal the surface. Where possible, use the special powder dyes, of which there is a huge range of colours. Mix them with bottled water to ensure a clean surface on your aluminium (but note that the powders are not intermixable). You should mix in the ratio of approximately one teaspoon of powder for every couple of litres of water. Do not breathe in the powder and keep the area well ventilated.

The dye solution used can also be reused until the dye is exhausted. Store any used dye in a clearly labelled container. Your dye bath should be at 40–50°C (104–122°F). Immerse some or all of your sheet in the bath for up to 10 minutes, depending on the strength of colour you want.

Finally, to seal the aluminium sheet, bring water to the boil, wait until it is properly boiling and immerse the sheet for a minimum of 45 minutes. The length of time will depend on the anodised layer, so check with the supplier. The colour is really in the metal now and is extremely resistant to anything except deep scratching.

FORMING

Aluminium work hardens and cannot be annealed once the colour has been dyed in the metal. This means it will have limitations on how it is formed. It can be pressed into shape with a mould and fly press or vice, or domed in a doming block, or shaped in a swage block. Use wooden punches and leather mallets, as it will mark easily and these marks cannot be removed. It is possible to texture the surface of the metal after it has been dyed, by passing the sheet through the rolling mill with paper or fabric.

The metal can be scored and bent but can only be moved into position once, as trying to move it back if you have gone too far will result in it breaking. Where it has been bent or curved, the anodised surface becomes cracked and crazed; if the stress has been too much this will affect the surface finish, but most of the time it is barely visible and gives the surface a bright sheen.

JOINING AND FIXING

It is possible to solder aluminium, but it is not easy. You can try out alternative methods of

ALWAYS WEAR PROTECTIVE GLOVES AND WORK IN A FUME CABINET OR WHERE THERE IS MOVING AIR.

Etched brooches, Jane Adam, 2000. Aluminium. Photo: Joël Degen.

joining by either pinning or riveting, or you can use epoxy adhesive or Superglue. Where possible, avoid joining two pieces of metal by glue alone; try to think of incorporating the fixture in the design where the design allows.

FINISHES

The sheet will already have either a shiny or matt finish and should not be touched after it has been dyed. If you attempt to polish it, the surface colour will be removed by the hard action of a polishing mop. Where files and papers have been used to smooth the edges of the metal, these edges will be undyed.

Ordinary aluminium can be etched to produce a textured or patterned surface. When using a diluted solution of ferric chloride, available from print suppliers, the solution must be *cold*, as the aluminium sheet will be completely eaten up in seconds if not. The process of etching generates heat anyway. Use a stop-out varnish and remember the back of your work. Have some small blocks of plastic in the bottom of the etch bath to raise the piece off the bottom. Use plastic tweezers or tongs to remove and rinse in water. Ordinary aluminium can be finished with fine wire wool, or else use a separate mop for polishing with a steel compound polish.

titanium

WHAT YOU WILL NEED

- ▶ lots of saw blades
- ▶ thick rubber gloves
- ▶ protective eyewear
- ▶ a glass dish
- ▶ titanium wire for an anode and cathode variable transformer (3–120 volts at 500 milliamps)
- ▶ ammonium sulphate (garden fertiliser).

HEALTH & SAFETY

Remember to work in a well-ventilated area.

Anodising titanium.
Photo: William Teakle.

MATERIALS

Titanium is a refractory metal belonging to a group that includes the metals niobium and tantalum. It has an extremely high melting point (1800°C/3272°F) and can maintain its strength when used at high temperatures. It is non-magnetic, lightweight and available in tube, rod, wire, mesh and sheet forms. It is not easy to work with, being a hard material, but for jewellery purposes the metal's great quality is its capability of being coloured, either through using heat or by electrolytic anodising.

CUTTING AND PIERCING

An ordinary jewellery piercing saw can be used, though due to titanium's hardness you may find that you get through quite a lot of blades. Drill using standard HSS drill bits.

JOINING AND FIXING

Titanium cannot be soldered but it can be joined to itself or another material using another softer metal as a pin or rivet. It can be TIG (tungsten inert gas) welded, but this is best done by someone with the relevant experience. Heat will affect the colour on the surface too, so where it has been welded the colour will have to be etched back. This is done using a highly dangerous acid, so again you may need another more experienced person to do this for you. Seek further advice from them.

FORMING

Titanium is not easily formed as the metal cannot be annealed, although it does work-harden which niobium does not. Titanium is most often lathe-formed in industry. Whereas most jewellers collect all silver and gold filings and scrap to be recycled and save money, titanium is a relatively inexpensive metal, and you can afford to lose some material as you work it . As titanium is hard to work, you can use a mandrel in a lathe chuck and turn a series of bangles from rod in a coil with a very slow running speed.

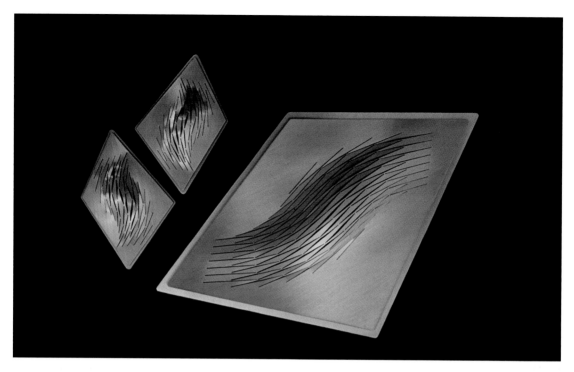

Slotted Brooches and Earrings, Ann Marie Shillito, 1995. Niobium and titanium. Photo: Ann Marie Shillito.

ANODISING

As mentioned above, titanium can be coloured using heat, and these colours are stable. With anodising, the colour in titanium is imparted by light being refracted through a layer of oxide on the metal's surface. The range of colours is similar to those of an oil spectrum. The particular colour seen by the eye is determined by the thickness of the oxide layer formed during, and the voltage used in, the anodising process. The oxide layer affects the way the light is reflected back off the surface of the metal and refracted through it to produce different wavelengths, thus altering the colour seen.

Clean the titanium, if possible with the highly dangerous acid, or if not, detergent to ensure bright colours. Prepare a bath of ammonium sulphate solution, around 20 g (1oz) of ammonium sulphate to 1 litre (33.8 fl.oz) of water. **Remember to wear strong rubber gloves.** The cathode wire (where the positive current flows out) is attached with a crocodile clip to the titanium, and the anode wire (where the positive current flows in) is placed in the solution. With this technique the titanium is held out of the solution. Vary the surface colour by adjusting the voltage, and grade the colours by bringing the metal out of the solution as the voltage is increased.

To vary the pattern created by the colours, try masking out specific areas. Use a stop-out resist similar to those used in etching. Masked areas will be lower-voltage colours, so start with the higher-voltage colours and then remove the masking material. The higher-voltage colours will not be affected when you anodise the unmasked area at a lower voltage. It is possible to attach the wire of the anode to the metal part of a paintbrush and dip the brush in the solution to produce a more painterly effect.

FINISHES

Once the colour has been applied to the surface, it cannot be worked on. The surface absorbs greases and after a period of time the colours may seem dull. Cleaning the piece in detergent can bring these colours back. The edges can be finished using files and papers.

copper & brass

WHAT YOU WILL NEED

- ▶ a plastic or glass container for the etching acid
- ▶ a feather
- ▶ plastic tweezers
- ▶ nitric acid
- ▶ fly press or large vice

HEALTH & SAFETY

Remember <u>a</u>lways to <u>a</u>dd <u>a</u>cid to water – AAA; adding water to acid causes a strong to violent reaction that could easily be dangerous to anyone standing nearby.

MATERIALS

In recent years, copper has become an increasingly costly metal to work in but it is still relatively inexpensive when compared with other metals. It is similar in hardness to sterling silver and is often used for working something out before the work is made again in silver. Most copper used for making purposes is cold-rolled and can be softened through annealing. The annealing temperature for copper is 600–700°C (1112–1292°F) and looks a deep pink colour; it can be quenched immediately. The melting temperature is 1080°C (1976°F).

Copper can be alloyed with other metals to produce altogether new metals in different colours and work hardnesses. Alloyed with silver it is known as shibuichi, a Japanese word, and produces a beautiful soft-pink colour; combined with gold it is known as shakudo and patinates a deep purple black. Brass is an alloy of copper and different amounts of other metals depending on the intended application. It is a hard material to work in. Zinc added in low quantities (a ratio of nine parts copper to one part zinc) makes the metal more workable and a more gold-like colour. Both copper and brass are available in wire, rod, tube, mesh and sheet form.

CUTTING AND PIERCING

Use either a piercing saw or snips to cut the metal, depending on the thickness of the sheet or stock. Drill copper or brass using a pillar drill or pendant motor and standard drill bits or burrs. Multiples of one shape in copper can be cut using the RT stamping system (see the *Glossary*).

JOINING AND FIXING

Copper and brass can be soldered using silver solders, though these do leave a white line; a less expensive alternative would be to use an 'easy flow' solder. Methods of joining the metal to itself or another

ALWAYS WEAR A CHARCOAL-FILTER MASK, RUBBER GLOVES, AN APRON AND GOGGLES. IF YOU DO NOT HAVE A FUME CABINET THEN WORK OUTSIDE AWAY FROM OTHERS OR IN AN AREA WITH MOVING AIR.

material without the use of heat would be to rivet, pin or stitch it with copper or brass wire. If you are using sheet metal, tabs can be cut into the metal and then thread or folded onto another piece of metal or other material.

FORMING

If you have had previous experience of working in silver then you will find that copper behaves in much the same way. Brass is harder, so some of the processes will take longer. Wire can be drawn down to size through a drawplate and sheet copper can be passed through a rolling mill. Try to use brass of the right size to avoid extra and difficult work.

Shape using pliers, mandrels and hammers. For a right angle bend use a scoring tool,this cuts a V-shape in the metal allowing a neat edge when folded.

Doming and swage blocks can be used to form the metal. Shapes can be pressed out into copper using a simple male and female mould using an acrylic or Tufnol mould.

FORGING

Both copper and brass can be hammered to shape a wire or rod or, using simple

silversmithing skills, sheet can be raised for larger, deeper shapes.

A hammering technique used on sheet metal, whereby only one edge of the metal is hammered, will stretch the metal in one area, moving it to create shape.

ETCHING

Etching can be used to create recessed areas in metal without tricky construction and soldering or a surface pattern. It is a simple process, though not without hazard on account of the acid chemicals used to etch away the metal. To etch copper, use water and nitric acid in a ratio of 1:1 **(see page 84 health and safety information)**. Other recipes can be used for different strengths of etching. Use all chemicals with the utmost care.

The metal should be cleaned with wet & dry papers. Carefully apply a stop-out solution to the metal, such as straw-hat varnish, leaving the area to be etched exposed; don't forget the back and sides of your piece. Next, immerse the piece in the etching solution and use a feather to brush away any bubbles. Remove the piece using plastic tweezers once it has been etched to the desired depth. Rinse well in cold running water. To remove the stop-out, clean the piece in turpentine.

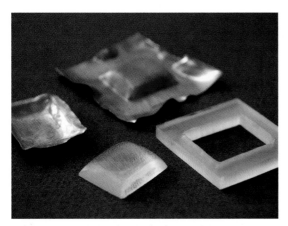

A simple press tool in acrylic or Tufnol; use 3–5mm thick depending on how deep a dome you want. Make sure the clearance between the male and female part is the same width as the metal to be pressed. Photo: William Teakle.

Etching copper; remember to stop out the back and sides. Work safely. Photo: William Teakle.

CREATIVE IDEA

Use copper to exploit its colour. Also, try making it behave more like a textile. Use mesh, or knit or weave fine copper wire.

REPOUSSAGE

This is a technique used to form a three-dimensional surface of bumps and lines in the metal by hammering it with small, shaped punches. To keep the work in position while shaping the metal, the sheet is placed onto a mixture of pitch, linseed oil and plaster powder contained in a metal bowl. The pitch content allows for the mixture to be warmed so that the metal can be removed or turned over.

FINISHES

File out any marks with normal jewellery files and use emery papers to reduce the marks on the metal. Try to limit the number of marks made in the metal as you work – as well as giving you less cleaning up to do, it stops the metal becoming overworked – unless you want a textured finish, in which case use an old hammer to give a hammered finish to the surface. A matt finish can be achieved by rubbing the surface with pumice powder, or a shiny polished one using either a polishing paste and cloth or a polishing motor with Tripoli, a compound for removing surface scratches before finishing with rouge. Use separate mops for each compound.

Test pieces showing work in copper wire and different surface finishes. Photo: William Teakle.

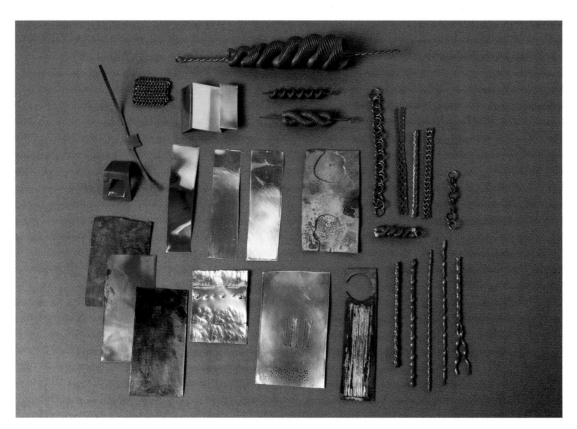

ENAMELLING

Copper can be enamelled using ground enamel powders and a small kiln. Refer to a book on enamelling as this is a specialist area. Remember that fittings must be soldered with enamelling solder or the joined pieces will come apart in the heat of the kiln.

PLATING AND ELECTROFORMING

A base-metal piece can be plated in silver or gold to keep the cost of materials down. A form of plating called electroforming uses copper in solution, which is precipitated by electricity out onto any other material. Natural objects such as seed-heads and leaves can also be coated in a layer of copper.

PATINATION

Unlike silver, copper and brass can be coloured using different chemical recipes to produce a range of surface colours. The use of these colours has to be carefully considered as they will wear off with time unless protected from constant contact with other surfaces. Copper can also be finished by simply quenching the piece in water while still red-hot. Try quenching in both cold and hot water; the black oxide layer will come off in flakes to reveal a bright-red patina. To stop it oxidising with the air again, spray or rub a thin film of wax on the surface. Copper cleaned in a pickle solution – the safest to use is safety pickle from jewellery tool suppliers – comes out a bright, light pinky colour. Again, this will react with the air and will slowly darken over time. This element of chance in how it ages could be an intended aspect of a piece's final appearance.

Unknown 4 Badge, Timothy Information Limited, 2007. Metal, paint. Photo: Simon Armitt.

steel

WHAT YOU WILL NEED

▸ use old pliers and files as steel is hard and could mark good tools

TIP

Types of carbon steel alloys:

Mild steel
low carbon content can be forged as more malleable when heated.

High carbon steel
used for springs and wires.

Steel is not immediately associated with jewellery but has been used for this purpose since as far back as the 17th century. Cut steel jewellery was made for several hundred years and evolved from buckle-making. Old horseshoe nails were melted and re-formed into studs, and these small pieces were cut to shape, or faceted and riveted, or screwed onto a baseplate. The steel beads or studs were then highly polished, producing something quite unique.

Steel is an alloy of mainly iron with up to 2% carbon by weight. It is one of the most common materials in the world. We would more usually associate steel with its huge range of industrial applications, including armoury, bathtubs and cars. It is possible to enamel steel, with the contrast of the dark metal looking great against the colourful enamel.

Stainless steel is an iron and carbon alloy with 11% chromium content. It does not rust or stain as easily as a carbon steel. Different grades are available depending on the application: austenitic or 300 series stainless steel has had nickel added to make it less brittle at lower temperatures. This is the best one to use for jewellery purposes: as the series number increases from 200 to 600, the different alloys each one refers to become harder to work.

Stainless steel is available in rod, sheet and wire form. Sprung

Soldering steel and using dental wire to make a brooch pin. Photo: William Teakle.

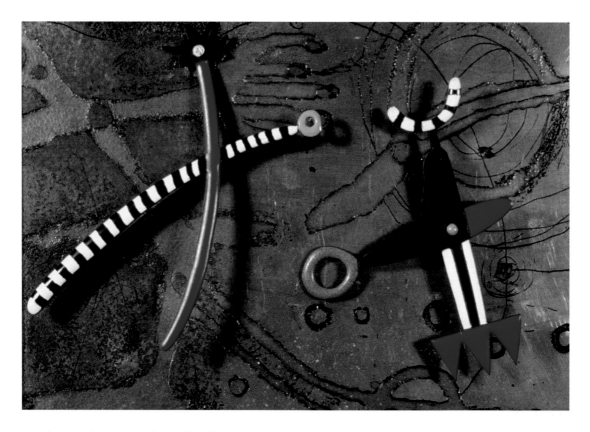

Brooches, Kim Ellwood, 1991.
Enamel, steel, gold leaf.
Photo: Abbott and Ellwood.

stainless-steel wire, mainly used in the dental industry, is very good for making brooch pins from, as well as being used creatively to make jewellery. It can be bought without already being hardened, making it easier to work with.

CUTTING AND PIERCING

Steel and stainless steel can be cut with a piercing saw, though it will soon dull the blades. Buy it in the size and thickness required, as it cannot be rolled any thinner. It can be drilled with HSS or cobalt drill bits, but lubricate well with oil and keep the drill speed slow; both the oil and the speed keep the temperature down and prevent the drill bit losing its cutting edge.

JOINING

Steel and stainless steel can be soldered using easy-silver solder and Easy-flo flux, or joined using a spot-welder. The area to be joined must be thoroughly cleaned and the soldering time kept as short as possible. Small portable single-phase, hand-operated spot-welders are available that can be used on steel wire and sheet. Other cold-connecting methods would be to rivet, pin or join the steel to itself by making a loop or jump-ring.

CREATIVE IDEA

Try using very thin sheet, making small multiple pieces attached to a frame or cloth to create a scale-like fabric piece. Try to make the hard look soft. Using very fine wire, bind or solder the steel together to form an organic or geometric shape. Dip-paint areas of the metal with enamel paints.

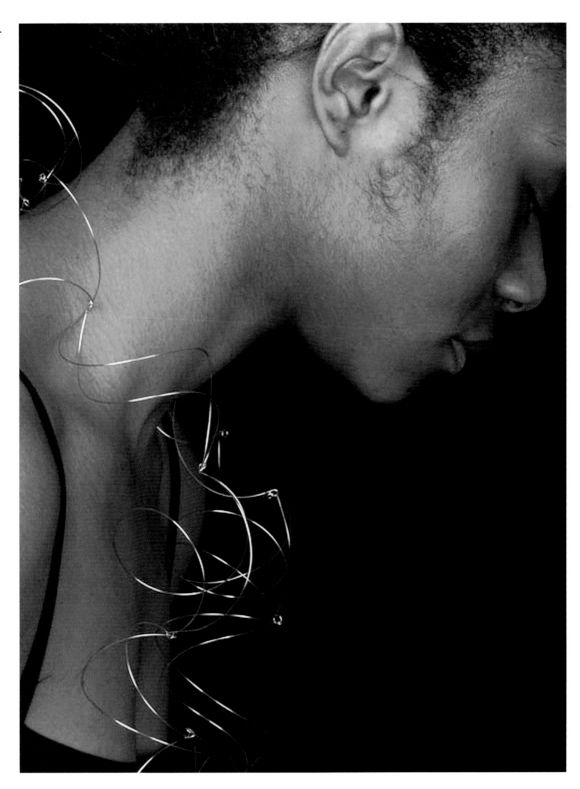

Doodle Chain, Gemma Farr, 2005. Steel wire. Photo: Gemma Farr.

FORMING

To shape the metal, rather than use a file it would be better to use an angle grinder with a grade of 60 grit. Stainless steel can be lathed using carbide tools. Some steels can be hot-forged to shape them, though you will need to find an anvil for this task.

FINISHING

Avoid using files that are used for other metals as any steel will blunt the file, with the result that it may not cut as well when then used to file another metal. Use emery papers to take out file marks and bring the steel up to the polishing stage. Use a hard polishing mop and stainless steel polishing compound.

tin

A silvery coloured metal with a low melting point that is not often used in jewellery, tin is very resistant to corrosion and retains its bright finish, and thus has been used to coat the outside of metals used to contain food. Copper, bronze and steel can all be hot-tinned, i.e. their surfaces coated in a thin layer of tin. Tin's malleability makes it easy to work with cold, but it does become brittle when heated. Tin is also widely used as a part of various alloys. Its melting point is low (231.9°C/449.4°F) and it casts well, which is why it is found in white-metal and pewter alloys.

One colourful use of tin or tinned metals is when it has been printed upon. However, fittings cannot be soldered on after a sheet has been printed, and thus are best incorporated in the metal and design of the piece.

SUGGESTIONS AND IDEAS

Before embarking on a particular technique in any of the metals, simply try working them in the state you bought them in. Use sheet, wire, tubing and rod. Start by piercing a pattern of lines or a series of different-sized drill holes, or using steel tools to punch patterns into the sheet material. To do this without a pitch bowl, work against a piece of wood or firm rubber, and find a variety of ways to bend up the metal into straight and curved shapes.

Cut lengths of wire and try different methods of using it, drawing with it by bending it with your fingers alone, or with pliers around formers or mandrels. Try soldering different thicknesses of wire. Alternatively, try joining wire without the use of solder. How many different ways can you do this?

the gallery

1	2	5
3	4	

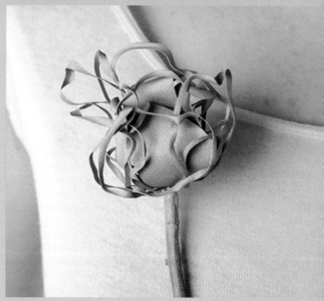

1 **Round Link Necklace**, Liana Pattihis, 2007. Enamelled copper mesh. Photo: Liana Pattihis.
2 **Pendant**, Debbie Long, 2007. Folded forged brass. Photo: Debbie Long.
3 **Flattened Brooch**, Lina Peterson, 2006. Gold-plated metal. Photo: Lina Peterson.
4 **Pink Rose Pin**, Zoë Newsome, 2007. Copper, cast bronze. Photo: Zoë Newsome.
5 **Flower Butterfly Brooch**, Melanie Tomlinson, 2005. Printed tin. Photo: Bogdan Tanea.

the gallery

	2	
1		4
	3	

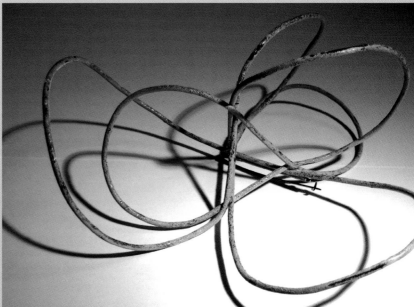

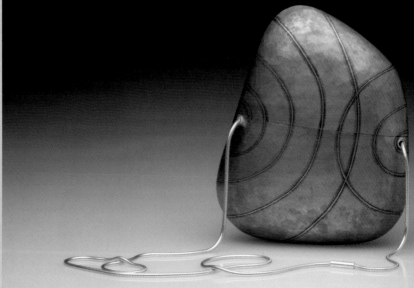

1 **Gardner Brooch,** Abbott and Ellwood, 2007.
Printed metal. Photo: Abbott and Ellwood.
2 **Green Spin Brooch**, Nicola Turnbull, 2007.
Brass, stainless steel. Photo: Nicola Turnbull.

3 **Small bag**, Jenifer Wall, 2002. Etched brass
Photo: Jerry Lebens.
4 **Green Piece**, Nan Nan Liu, 2007. Copper, gilding metal.
Photo: Nan Nan Lui.

8. stone, bone, & other materials

Stone and bone have been used for many thousands of years to create tools and implements, as well as decorative pieces, and can be equally effective used in contemporary jewellery. Returning to natural materials and recycling used materials has become more popular as environmental issues become more of a concern. Non-precious stones that have been used in contemporary jewellery include marble and granite, as well as found geological stone. Often one has to wet the surface to reveal a stone's full potential, and it usually needs to be cut and worked to permanently bring out its characteristics. Ivory is no longer used as the animals from which it is derived are endangered. Unlike ivory, bone can be a by-product of another process. The same with horns or antlers, some of which are naturally shed and it is these that should be used. As a material, horn of different animals varies greatly in appearance and density, with some being a modified form of bone and pure horn being derived from skin. Other materials that can be used will depend upon your approach to making and designing a piece. An example of a highly original approach to material was a series of vases 'made' by Tomás Gabzdil Libertiny who fabricated a vase-shaped hive which bees then colonised, building a wax honeycomb within the shape. After a week, the 40,000 bees were then moved into a new hive, leaving behind a quite incredible vase, which particularly when the process behind how it is made is unknown, is a wonder to look at.

1 **necklace (back),** Charlotte de Syllas, 2005.
Cachalong, polyester braid, gold. Photo: David Cripps.
2 **necklace (front),** Charlotte de Syllas, 2005.
Cachalong, polyester braid, gold. Photo: David Cripps.
3 **Kiss Neckpiece,** Elisabeth Gilmour, 2005.
Porcelain. Photo: Richard Coop.

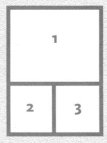

1	
2	3

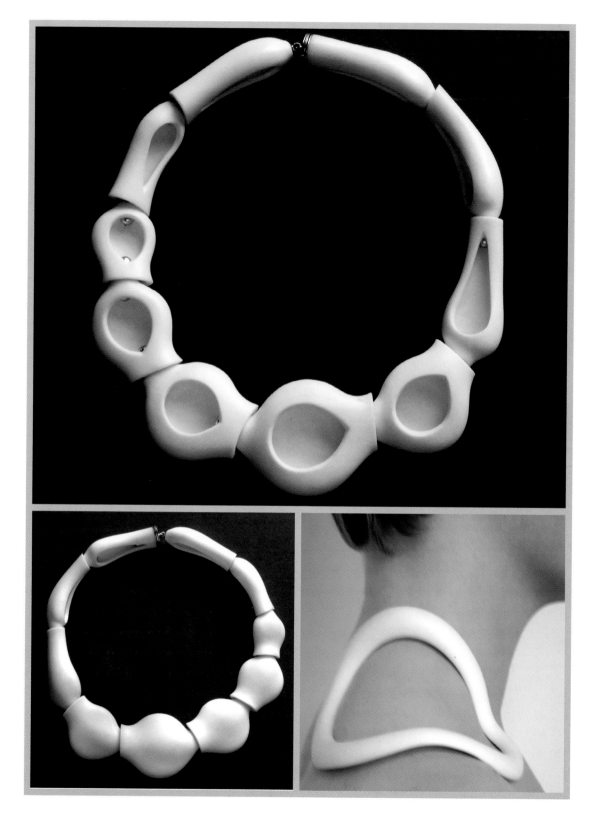

stone

WHAT YOU WILL NEED

▸ diamond-coated papers, files and drill bits

▸ wet & dry papers

▸ a diamond-edged circular saw

▸ lapping plate

TIPS

Test as many different samples of stone as you can, simply by cutting, piercing and gluing them. Keep notes.

Carve the surface with burrs to produce texture, or pierce a thin piece to make a filigree-like item. How thin can the material go before it breaks?

MATERIALS

Stones do vary in hardness, but as materials go stones are hard to work and require special diamond tools to cut and shape them, though this need not be as expensive as you might imagine as the diamonds in question are industrial ones. You can save money, too, by using marble or granite offcuts or broken bits from marble manufacturers, as well as old bricks and found pebbles.

When choosing a stone with which to work, look carefully for interesting colour, inclusions and shapes, and work out where you will cut it to make the shape you require. One piece may be better than another. Be aware that some of the inclusions may be far harder or softer than the stone around them.

CUTTING AND PIERCING

The best way to cut stone is with a diamond-edged circular saw that rotates over a bed of water. In fact, the saw grinds the material rather than cuts it. All cutting or piercing of stone has to be done wet so as to remove the fine debris safely, and it also helps to cool the cutting tool. Hold small pieces of stone in a jig or clamp. Make sure the work stays wet, and feed the stone at a slow speed to avoid chipping and shattering the final edge. Use a wooden pusher when the work gets close to the blade; it helps disperse the vibrations. It is possible to get different thicknesses of saw blade, but they are not very fine; take this into account when you are working out the cutting lines. For smaller, more delicate work, there is a cutting tool that will fit in a pendant drill. Again, work wet, use a shallow basin filled with water and keep the work and cutting bit just below the surface. This makes it slightly easier to see what you are doing, though it is also worth checking progress on a regular basis. Cutting the surface, and some shaping, can be done using diamond-coated dental burrs and collars, but once again, you should work in water.

To drill a hole in stone, you should use special diamond-coated twist drill bits, though a hole can also be made with a round burr

TAKE EXTRA CARE WHEN USING ELECTRIC MACHINES WITH WATER. WEAR RUBBER SHOES AND A LARGE APRON WHEN CUTTING STONE.

(albeit less accurately and only if the stone is not too thick, as the collar of the burr may be larger than the hole made). These, too, must be used in water. For larger holes you'll need to find a diamond-core drill, which is sometimes used in the glass industry or by marble manufacturers. These cut larger holes by removing a line of material around the circumference of the hole and leaving a core slightly smaller than the hole drilled.

SHAPING

Once the basic shape of the stone has been cut, the rest of the material can be removed using diamond grit papers stuck to a flat, half-round or round stick. These are available in different grades; start coarse and work through the grades to fine so as to remove all cutting marks. Where a lot of material needs to be taken away, a lapping machine or grinding wheel are much less time-consuming. They are not easy to find second-hand, but not impossible. Check with the suppliers and the association mentioned at the back of the book.

JOINING AND FIXING

Whether you are joining stone to itself or to another material, a good epoxy glue will work best. Remember that some stones are more porous than others, and a thin glue will travel or move away from the join by capillary action. When used on a coloured stone, you can add colour to the adhesive

Cutting stone using a diamond edged circular saw. Photo: William Teakle

Above: Shaping the stone on a lapping machine using diamond-coated paper. This can also be done on a grinding wheel and by hand using different grades of diamond and wet and dry papers. Photo: William Teakle.

Left: Drilling a hole with a diamond twist drill. Always work under water and with great care where water and electricity are combined. Photo: William Teakle.

Square Knotted Necklace, Maike
Barteldres, 2005. Sandstone, linen.
Photo: Jason Ingram.

TIPS

Some types of marble
can be dyed, producing
brightly coloured veins.
Hot clothing-dye is quite
well-suited to this
purpose.

Some stones can have
metal soldered near
them without any
consequence. Test first.

Come up with six
different methods of
joining one piece of
shaped stone to another.

to disguise the join, but do so sparingly as too much
added colour will inhibit the strength of the bond.
Minuscule amounts of resin paste or oil paint
would suit this purpose.

For jewellery purposes, the stone should
not be so large that the piece becomes too
heavy to wear. This consideration can make it
tricky in cases where you may need to drill a
hole so that you can pin pieces together. If the
material around the hole is too thin then the
hole will shatter and chip. One solution is to
drill the hole where you need it before
removing the surrounding material. Make sure
all the debris is cleaned out of the hole, which
should also be dry before you insert the pin
you intend to glue. Roughen the surface of the
pin to increase adhesion.

FINISHES

Very fine wet & dry papers are enough to produce
a really smooth, almost polished finish on stone
surfaces. If you wanted a highly polished surface,
micromesh or a stone-polishing machine can be
used. Stones are placed in a barrel with fine
cutting powders; again, these come in various
grades and polish by attrition, a little like the
action of the waves on a beach. However,
problems may well arise with soft stones polished
in this way, as the rough and tumble of a polishing
machine could lead to chipping, which would be
hugely frustrating after all the effort involved in
making a piece. With porous stones, the surface
can be sealed with a light film of wax. Tests of
different sorts will need to be carried out on the
stone type used before you start work.

NON-PRECIOUS JEWELLERY

bone & horn

WHAT YOU WILL NEED

- a chemist's supply of hydrogen peroxide (3%)
- a steel tool
- some inks

TIP

Try marking the surface as if it was a scrimshaw piece. Use a sharp steel tool to engrave the surface. Indian ink or dye colours can be rubbed into the engraved line.

By what methods other than adhesive can you join bone to other materials?

Find ways of using the percussive sound of bone within a piece of jewellery.

MATERIALS

These are not materials immediately associated with jewellery, and their use may also upset some people, so it is worth making the point that no animal should be killed just for its bone or horn. Nevertheless, these are materials that have been used for thousands of years to make a variety of everyday objects – combs, drinking vessels and corset stays, to name a few – and are still being used by luthiers and other fine instrument makers. Taken to another level, more recently is the work of some jewellers from the Royal College of Art, who have collaborated with medical researchers to grow human bone rings. Volunteers donated bone and marrow to them, and this was then used in a laboratory to grow more bone in the shape of a ring. One volunteer particularly liked the idea of wearing a very real part of their partner at all times. These materials are lighter to hold than expected, and warm to the touch.

PREPARING

The best sort of bone to use initially would be that of a cow, as its density, size and limited marrow cavity make it ideal. Ask your local butcher for a section of long shin bone (a prize bull produces the densest bone). It is essential that the bone is prepared very carefully, as any remaining grease can impair the work, including its other component materials, at a later date. Do not boil or bleach bone; chlorine-based bleach damages the bone, making it weak and porous.

The following is the simplest method of cleaning bone, using bacterial action. First remove as much soft tissue as possible from the cavity and surface, using a scraper if necessary. Surface grease can be removed with household ammonia **(though this does require very good ventilation)**. Rinse the bone well before proceeding, then immerse it in a container of water and place this somewhere warm where the smell will not disturb anyone. Change the water daily; the mucky, greasy water can be poured on the garden. When the water finally stays clear overnight, the bacteria will have done their job.

Next, soak the bone in hydrogen peroxide obtained from a chemist until the bone reaches the shade of white you prefer. This will also sterilise the bone. Finally, leave to air-dry for a couple of days and then cut to the required size.

Another kind of bone that could be used comes from shed antlers, which are not horn as is commonly believed.

Dust to Dust Rings, Kelly McCallum, 2006. Human bone, live plant. Photo: Kelly McCallum.

CUTTING AND FORMING

First of all, when using bone, work wet as much as possible, as bone dust is dangerous to breathe in. Bone can be cut or pierced using a band saw or piercing saw, or else ordinary drill bits and burrs. Note that as you work with bone, it will smell of burning hair.

SHAPING AND FORMING

The shape and size of the material will dictate what you can achieve. You should use old files which are fairly coarse or files kept only for this purpose. Some removal of material to shape the bone can be done on the linisher, but be aware of porous areas. **Wear a mask and attach an extractor to the machine.** Smaller or fragile areas can be done with wet & dry paper. Any staining can be overcome by returning the piece to the hydrogen peroxide solution.

Horn is a natural thermoplastic and in the 1900s was shaped by heat and pressure in a mould (see the earlier Plastics section).

JOINING AND FIXING

Slow-cure epoxy adhesive will join bone to itself or other materials, though it may require some pinning to hold the pieces in position. Try out different adhesives and epoxy resins.

FINISHES

Work through the grades of finishing paper up to the finest grade possible to achieve the surface finish you want. Bone will polish slightly, though not brightly; the surface should be sealed with a wax spray to avoid being discoloured by grease.

other materials

There are many materials I have not mentioned, but this should not stop you from finding out about them or using them for jewellery. Techniques and methods from other craft and art disciplines can be adapted to jewellery. Sometimes seemingly fragile materials such as porcelain and glass have been used to great effect in jewellery. Otherwise, use what is around you, recycle what you find and turn it into something unexpected. The simplest object can be transformed into a wearable piece of jewellery. You may want to retain an element of its origin or you may want to make it disappear. It's up to you.

Amulet series, Stina Lind, 2007. Porcelain, acrylic, string. Photo: Stina Lind.

the gallery

1 **Plastic Bottle Necklace (detail**), Samantha Queen, 2007.
  Plastic bottle and bamboo. Photo: Samantha Queen.
2 **Demipe 1–3,** Ute Eitzenhöfer, 2002. Plastic packaging caps.
  Photo: Ute Eitzenhöfer.
3 **Home for the Wrist,** Caroline Holt, 2007. Bone, resin.
  Photo: Caroline Holt.
4 **Fanciful,** Joanna Tinker, 2005. Plastic carrier bags.
  Photo: J. Tinker.

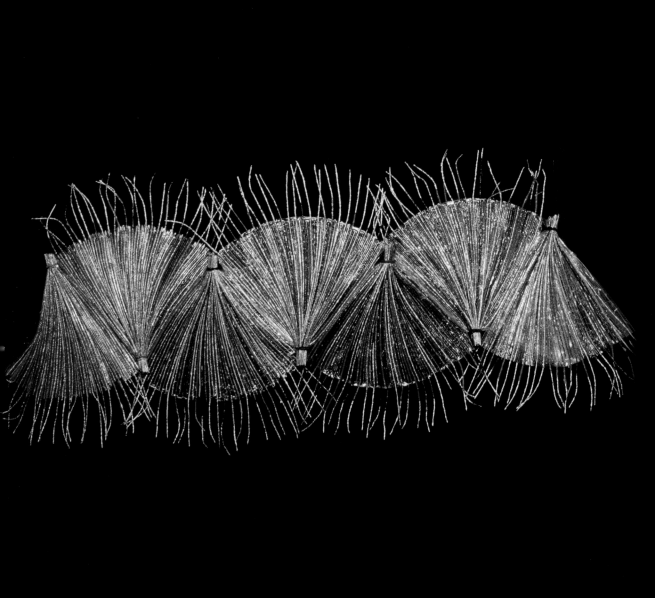

9. design & make briefs

Having played around with some of the non-precious materials in this book, the following briefs have been devised to help you produce a finished piece. This is the hardest part, combining your own visual research with the knowledge gained about a material, using aspects of what you've discovered through experimentation to come up with a design, which you then have to execute.

The first thing to say is that you should keep things as simple as possible. Try to keep within your own technical ability, and ideas will evolve. Start by sketching out initial ideas as a reaction to the brief, by looking at your material samples and by reckoning what you can achieve in the material. When you are designing, you should keep in mind the **form** and **shape**, and its **function**, how the **process** of using your chosen material will work, and whether one thing has to be completed before you can realise another stage, bearing in mind that they are not always in the order you might expect: **surface finish, texture** and **colour**. Remember that the finish and quality of the back should be as good as the front. Don't just stick on a fitting; think about how it works with the whole.

Make small maquettes, or models, out of paper, string and card or Plasticine. Seeing something three-dimensionally in card or Plasticine can make a huge difference. Decide on a design you like and carry it out. It's quite likely to change as it is made, but remember it is the quality of finish and the attention to detail that is so important, not whether it looks exactly like the sketch. Sometimes as you are making one design, other ideas for pieces come about.

New designs often emerge from the visual notebook you should keep, but they also come from the material as you are working on it. Much less often, a maker will set themselves a brief, or even less frequently they'll receive a commission in which the brief is presented to them. Designing within someone else's parameters can help to get you to think and make in a different way, which can be both frustrating and liberating at the same time. Whatever the starting point, it's important always to finish your work to the highest possible standard – you must be your harshest critic – but above all to have fun.

All of the briefs in this chapter can be applied to the other forms of jewellery described, so by all means make a bangle instead of earrings where it suits.

TIP
Magnets make good hidden catches.

DESIGN BRIEF ONE

Design and make a *necklace* from a chosen material, forming each element of the necklace using a curling technique. The material should curl back around on itself, and can either be fixed in position or left under tension.

Points to consider: How long will the necklace be? How do you connect the repeated shapes? Will they interlock or be strung like a bead? What is the material they would be strung on? Is there a catch? Can you design it to be an integral part of the necklace? Also consider the finish. If the ends are left open, make sure they don't snag on clothing.

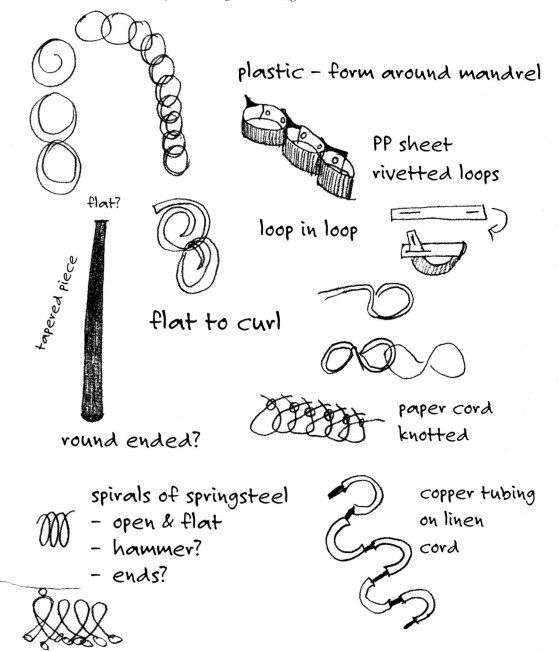

flat?

plastic – form around mandrel

PP sheet
rivetted loops

loop in loop

tapered piece

flat to curl

round ended?

paper cord
knotted

spirals of springsteel
– open & flat
– hammer?
– ends?

copper tubing
on linen
cord

TIP

The size of the inside diameter for the average wrist is between 6 cm (2.4 in.) and 6.5 cm (2.6 in.).

DESIGN BRIEF TWO

Design and make a *bangle* or *bracelet* starting with the notion that the wrist is not round. How do you make a shape you can get onto your wrist over your hand? Use a flexible material such as rubber, cloth or paper. How does the material you use dictate the shape of the outside of the bangle or bracelet?

Points to consider: If it is a bracelet, how does the catch work?

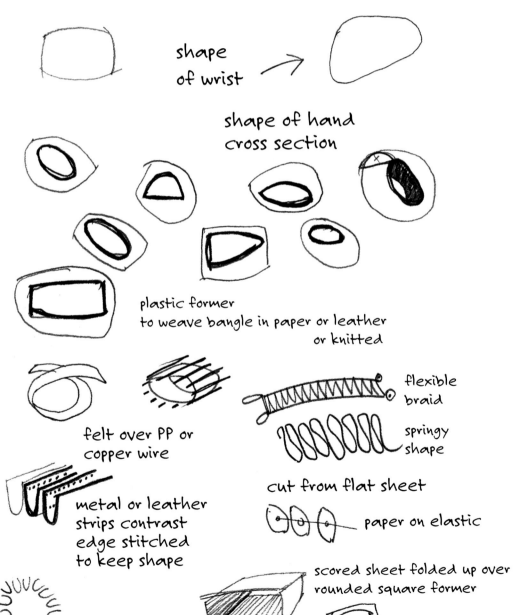

shape of wrist →

shape of hand cross section

plastic former to weave bangle in paper or leather or knitted

felt over PP or copper wire

flexible braid

springy shape

cut from flat sheet

paper on elastic

metal or leather strips contrast edge stitched to keep shape

scored sheet folded up over rounded square former

DESIGN BRIEF THREE

Design and make a *brooch* using the imagery of signs and symbols. From your research and drawings, choose an idea and combine two different materials. This project would be an ideal opportunity to introduce colour or surface texture.

Points to consider: How will the fitting work and will there be a safety catch? Try making your own rather than using a bought catch. If the material used cannot be soldered, how does the fitting attach? Make it a part of the design.

TIP

Brooch-fitting catch openings should face downwards.

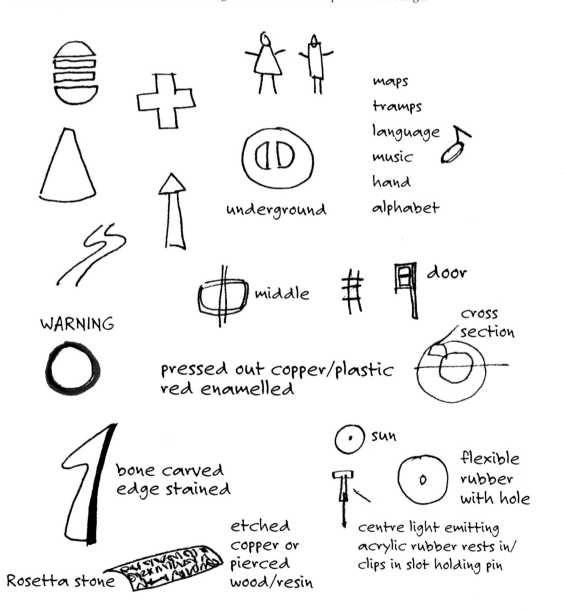

maps
tramps
language
music
hand
alphabet

underground

middle

door

cross section

WARNING

pressed out copper/plastic red enamelled

bone carved edge stained

Rosetta stone

etched copper or pierced wood/resin

sun

flexible rubber with hole

centre light emitting acrylic rubber rests in/ clips in slot holding pin

TIP

An ear-wire for pierced ears is around 0.8–1 mm (0.03–0.04in.) depending on the wearer's preference.

DESIGN BRIEF FOUR

Design and make *a pair of earrings* using wire, tubing, cord or thin strips of material. Use various techniques depending on the material chosen, to make an open, structured pair of earrings. Make them quite large as the lack of weight will allow the design to be a little more extrovert.

Points to consider: Where will the ear-wire fit on the design? Will it be a geometric or an organic structure? Draw on visual information of buildings or plants.

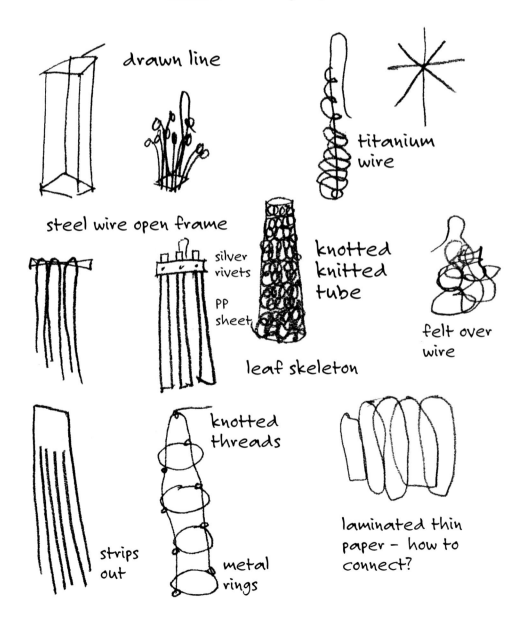

drawn line

titanium wire

steel wire open frame

silver rivets

PP sheet

knotted knitted tube

felt over wire

leaf skeleton

strips out

knotted threads

metal rings

laminated thin paper – how to connect?

DESIGN BRIEF FIVE

Design and make a *ring* in which the material tells a story. It could be a marble chip from an old floor, a piece of wood from a walk, a drinks can from a reunion with an old friend, paper from your favourite childhood book or copper from an old piece of plumbing. Then associate that material with something else, such as enamelled badges and medals, or with medical, historical or political uses.

Points to consider: Find things in your immediate vicinity or reclaim and recycle.

TIP

With a wider ring shank, it is best to make it a size or two larger than the wearer's ring size. Always measure the size from the centre of the ring.

carved stone

copper tubing squashed

paper book leaves

pulped paper from show ticket set in mould

leather

pieces of found plastic heat fused & squashed

ring of felt balls

old jumper

old plastic/horn comb

favourite leather shoe

glossary

Acetate Clear sheet, available in different thicknesses from art/craft shops, onto which you can photocopy.

Acetone A highly flammable, volatile, colourless liquid used to clean up certain adhesives, though it may leave a mark. It dissolves the surface of cellulose acetate and this can be used to weld pieces together. It will also clean up uncured polyester resin. Store with care and use in a well-ventilated area.

Alloy A compound metal such as brass, gilding metal or bronze, created by melting together two or more pure metals.

Ammonium sulphate A salt compound commonly used as a fertiliser, and also in solution to anodise titanium.

Anneal To heat metal so as to soften it and make it workable.

Anodise To apply an oxide layer to the surface of aluminium or titanium.

Awl A tool with a pointed steel spike for marking holes in wood or leather, or scoring lines in paper without cutting it.

Batt A fluffy sheet of uncombed but carded wool.

Belt sander A machine with a continuous loop belt of grit paper which rotates rapidly and speeds up the process of removing material. Also known as a linisher.

Bench drill A smaller, tabletop version of a pillar drill, used for drilling smaller pieces of plastic, wood or metal.

Burnishing Polishing a surface or edge by rubbing it with a special tool.

Burr (see also **Dental burr**) A small amount of debris material, created along a pierced line or around a drilled hole, which remains attached to the main material body.

Calibrated cup Clear plastic (polypropylene) cup with graded millilitre marks.

Carded A term used to describe wool that has been combed out to separate the fibres.

Cascamite Powdered resin glue to which you add water and when dry, forms a waterproof bond.

Cast A process by which a liquid material is set solid in a mould so as to shape it.

Catalyst A substance added to rubber or resin in small quantities to initiate polymerisation or a chemical reaction.

Chasing A technique for creating a raised surface on metal using steel tools.

Coarse blades Piercing-saw blades size 2–4 .

Coarse files For example, a bastard-cut file 15–25 cm (6–10 in.) in length, flat or half-round.

Couching mound A pile of wet folded newspapers or towels in a tray with sides, which is covered with a kitchen cloth, onto which handmade paper is released, or couched, from its moulding frame.

Curing The process by which plastic or rubber fully hardens during the process of turning into a solid.

Cutting mat A specialised rubber mat that enables you to cut paper and other material accurately without damaging your work surface.

Cyanoacrylate see **Superglue**.

Dental burr or **rotary cutting burr** A small cutting tool used in a pendant drill, available in different shapes – ball, cone and others. The surface of the burr has many cutting edges and is used to remove material.

Dispersol/disperse dye Used for dyeing synthetics such as plastic.

Draw To pull or stretch a material over a mould to create depth.

Draw plate A steel plate with holes of various sizes through which annealed metal wire can be pulled to make it a smaller (diameter) thickness. The plates come with different shaped holes.

Dye bath A container in which a solution of dye colour is heated, into which is placed the object to be dyed, usually stainless steel to avoid contamination.

Emboss To raise the surface of a ductile material using a die or metal pattern onto which the material is pressed.

Emery paper Paper coated with different grades of emery grit used to remove file marks from metalwork. Cannot be used with water.

Engrave To cut a line in the surface of a material with a metal tool or graver.

Epoxy A two-part glue such as Araldite or a type of two-part resin that is mixed together to set hard.

Etching A process by which material is eaten away by contact with an acid or other chemical.

Exothermic reaction A chemical reaction that gives off heat. Most resins generate heat as they react with the catalyst during the curing process.

Extruded Describes material which has been shaped into long sections by pushing or drawing it through a die or a shaped hole.

Female shape A negative shape or space in a mould.

Ferric chloride Used in printing, a chemical that etches a metal surface. Always use with great care.

Fly press A screw-type press that can be operated manually, where the flywheel or weight arm attached to the screw produces the driving force.

Flux Paste or medium used to prevent metal oxidising when being soldered.

Foam core A board made of plastic foam that is sandwiched in between paper or card.

Former A shape made of metal, wood or other material, used to shape a softer material around or over its own form.

Fulling The process that thickens the felt during the making.

Gel The stage at which resin turns from liquid to solid and forms a jellylike substance.

Gelflex The brand name for a re-meltable PVC rubber used in mould-making.

Gilding metal An alloy of copper and zinc, a type of brass.

Half-hitch knot A simple knot where one end of a rope loops once around the other end and is pulled back through the loop.

Hardener A chemical used to trigger the reaction that turns a material such as resin or rubber into a solid.

Hotplate An electrically heated ring for heating up containers of liquid.

Hot-air gun A handheld tool which is usually used to strip paint but can be used to heat small thermoplastic pieces in order to bend or form them, or localised heating on a larger piece of thermoplastic.

Hot-glue gun A tool which electrically heats round sticks of plastic based adhesive, that is pushed by a trigger mechanism in a controlled stream, hardens on cooling. Good for quick temporary fixing.

Hydrogen peroxide A weak acid with strong oxidising properties which acts as a bleaching agent.

Jig A device for holding a piece securely while it is being worked on with another tool.

Jigsaw A mechanised coarse saw blade used for cutting curves in materials such as wood or plastic.

Keyed finish The surface of a material roughened to allow for better adhesion at the point of contact with the glue.

Laminate To stick layers of a material(s) together.

Lathe A machine that rotates a piece of material (at speeds which can be varied) in order to cut a symmetrical surface using a tool that runs parallel and at angles to the spinning work. The material to be cut is held in a chuck.

Lay-up The process of preparing and curing one layer of rubber or resin so that another layer can be poured or applied on top.

Linisher See **Belt sander**.

Linocut Pieces of printing lino (similar to linoleum flooring material) cut away or engraved to leave a picture or pattern in the raised areas, linocuts are then inked and pressure is applied to transfer the image to paper or another sheet material.

Male shape A positive shape or space in a mould.

Mandrel A conical tool made of steel or another hard material, used to shape another, softer material in circles or curves.

Marquetry A decorative craft in which a thin veneer of a material, usually wood, is used to cover the surface of an object.

Master The original form or shape used to create the female shape in a mould.

Micromesh An abrasive cloth with finer grades than wet & dry paper, used to finish the surface of a variety of materials.

Monofilament A manmade fibre or line made with one strand – for instance, nylon line used in fishing line or in stringing tennis rackets.

Muslin A fine cotton cloth.

Nitric acid A strong acid used to etch copper and silver. **Wear rubber gloves and eye protection, as well as a rubber apron to prevent holes in your clothes. Use in a fume cabinet or a well-ventilated area.**

Overlocking A sewing-machine term, also known as 'serging', denoting where the edge of the fabric is sewn to prevent fraying.

Oxidised Where a metal has reacted with oxygen in the air to produce a thin layer of an oxide of that material. This can be beneficial in the case of aluminium and titanium, or not where the oxide layer tarnishes the metal, such as with copper or brass. Oxidising can be controlled and applied to some effect, such as when using a solution of liver of sulphur to turn the surface of copper a deep black.

Pendant drill A handheld flexible shaft drill used by jewellers, with different tools for drilling, burring and finishing.

Piercing Refers to cutting out material using a jeweller's piercing saw with fine and coarse blades; also, where the surface of a material is pierced to create a hole by drilling or burring.

Piercing saw A jeweller's saw used with blades ranging from coarse to fine. For the purposes of this book and the materials used, coarse refers to 2–4 and fine 0–4/0.

Pillar drill A free-standing drill used for drilling large pieces of material.

Pinning A technique for holding together material such as wood or plastic by the use of adhesive and fine metal pins, either visible or hidden within the object. Gives strength to a join.

Pitchbowl A metal bowl containing pitch, linseed oil and plaster powder, used in repoussage and in chasing.

Plycord Cord made using a number of strands of fibre. The number, for instance 2-ply or 4-ply, refers to the number of strands used.

Polymer A chemical compound whose molecule is comprised of a chain of smaller repeated monomer units. Often refers to plastics but actually denotes a large number of natural and synthetic materials.

Pot time Refers to the available working time once two-part materials such as rubbers or resins have been mixed together before the compound starts to set and becomes unpourable or unworkable.

Procion dyes Powder dyes dissolved in water and used hot to dye natural materials. They take well on cellulose-based materials such as cotton, linen, viscose, rayon and wood.

Pulp A soft mass of pulverised wood or fabric, used in making paper.

Pumice powder Abrasive grit of pumice stone in fine powder form, available in different grades for applying a fine matt finish to the surface of a material. It can be used in a barrel polisher with ceramic or stone chips, but not steel shot.

PVC Abbreviation for polyvinyl chloride, a type of plastic.

PVA Polyvinyl acetate is an emulsion in water used as an adhesive for porous materials, particularly wood, paper and cloth. The most commonly used wood glue, it will also seal porous surfaces on masters used in silicone-rubber mould-making.

Pyrography A technique whereby a heated tool is used to burn a pattern or image into the surface of wood.

Quenched When heated metal has been cooled in water or pickle to remove the oxidised surface.

Repoussage The process of hammering out or pressing thin metal from the reverse side.

Resist A liquid or material applied to another material's surface to prevent a chemical or dye from altering the original or coloured surface while another process is applied to that surface. Used in etching and dyeing.

Rifflers A double-ended handheld tool similar to a file, in grades ranging from coarse to very fine, used for removing material in awkward places. The ends come in a wide variety of shapes and curves.

Rolling mill A hand-operated machine in a jeweller's workshop that alters the thickness of a material, usually sheet metal, by passing it through two parallel steel rollers, which force the material to stretch and change thickness.

Roving Wool fibre which has been combed so that all the fine strands lie in the same direction.

RT stamping system A patented system designed for making a cutting tool with a scissor-like action. Very useful for cutting out multiples of a variety of thin sheet materials ranging from paper to aluminium (see paper and leather suppliers).

Scalpel A very accurate and sharp craft knife used for cutting fine lines or shaving off material. Different-shaped blades are available, similar to those used by surgeons.

Scored Where a small line of material is removed with a tool to allow for a clean bend in the material.

Screen-printing A method by which an image is transferred to a sheet material by pressing inks through a fine screen-mesh stencil.

Shelf life The time for which a material can be stored before it will no longer be effective or usable.

Shellac The brittle secretion of an insect, collected from the bark of trees on which the insect lives; it is a naturally

occurring polymer and is used in solution, mainly on wood, as a hard, water-repellent varnish.

Silicone rubber A material used to make accurate, flexible and firm moulds for casting resin or pewter. A cold-casting material that can withstand high temperatures, it can also be used as a material in its own right.

Single phase Means a machine that is single phase can be plugged into a normal domestic electrical-supply system. Used to distinguish from three-phase electric machines, which use an industrial electrical supply.

Skin Refers to a thin layer of rubber moulding material pasted over a master shape. It can help you to use less rubber over a large or deeply undercut surface.

Snips A handheld but not very accurate tool for cutting metal.

Solder To join metal together using an alloy with a lower melting point than the metal pieces being joined, using heat from a gas torch and flux to allow the solder to flow.

Stock Refers to the industrial forms in which a material is available, such as rod, sheet, tube or wire, in various profiles (round, half-round, square or cross-section).

Stop-out See **Resist**

Stringing Using a cord or thread to join beads in a line. Depending on the size of the bead, the cord or thread is knotted between each bead.

Superglue Also known as cyanoacrylate, a powerful adhesive when used in the correct way, though it must be used with care as it can permanently stick skin together. However, it does eventually become water-soluble and can be a bit brittle.

Swage block A steel block with U-shaped grooves used to shape sheet metal into U-shapes or when starting to turn it into tubing. It can be used for plastic.

Swarf Loose waste material, sometimes occurring in lengths, the result of latheing, drilling or cutting.

Tatting A textile technique that produces a large lacelike structure comprised of a series of knots and loops.

Tensile strength The strength of force that can be applied to a material being stretching before it breaks.

Tensol cement An adhesive used on some plastics. It is a solvent cement (dichloromethane) that dissolves the surface layers of a wide range of thermoplastics. The solvent evaporates, leaving a joint similar to a weld, made from an intermingling of the two plastic melted surfaces. The pieces to be adhered should be clamped for 24 hours to ensure a permanent joint. Acrylic is usually joined with Tensol cement, and high-impact polystyrene and PVC are also joined by solvent cements. Polythene and polypropylene cannot be glued by solvent welding because they will not dissolve in any solvent. Thermosetting plastics cannot be glued by this process either.

Thermoplastic A type of plastic that can be heated and formed, which will then revert to its original shape if heated again.

Thermosetting plastic A type of plastic that undergoes a single irreversible change through heat and sometimes pressure to form a solid.

Thixotropic Describes the thick, unpourable consistency of a liquid.

TIG (tungsten inert gas) welding Produces clean, precise welds on any metal. A tungsten electrode heats the metal you are welding, and a gas (usually argon) protects the melted metal from contamination. Get a specialised TIG welder to do

the work as a protective mask with a tinted eye-filter glass needs to be worn.

Toner A powder used in laser printers and photocopiers to form the text and images on the printed paper or acetate. It can be transferred from the paper or acetate to a plastic or metal sheet and will act as a resist, though it will also tend to rub off.

Tufnol A reinforced, laminated plastic engineering material that can be used for making press tools. Check with the supplier over the correct one for your use.

Vacuum machine Equipment to extract all air from a liquid material, used in particular when casting bio resin.

Ventilation Allows fresh air continually to circulate, thereby rapidly dissipating any fumes or odours. A portable machine can be bought which can pull in fresh air and blow it into a room that lacks adequate ventilation.

Vice A device for holding work firmly, leaving hands free to use tools or machinery.

Vinamould A re-meltable plastic rubber material used for mould-making and resin-casting.

Visual diary For the purposes of this book, this refers to a collection of observed drawings,

images from magazines, photographs, notes and objects that can be collated in a sketchbook or stuck on a wall, board or shelf. These are used as reference and inspirational material to influence your own design voice.

Wad punch Also called a paper drill, a tubular steel tool for making clean-edged holes without the need to drill in a thin material such as leather, plastic, card, paper or cloth.

Warp A weaving term, it means the set of lengthwise yarns through which the weft is woven to make cloth.

Warping The distortion of a flat sheet of material caused by heat or damp.

Weld To join two pieces of the same material by melting the surface of the pieces to be joined and allowing them to amalgamate and then cool.

Wetting agent A chemical that increases the spreading and penetration of a liquid, used particularly in dyeing to increase uptake of dye colour by a material.

Work-harden As a metal is worked on by hammering, forming and bending, the material becomes unmalleable. To soften it again, it should be annealed.

suppliers

rubber suppliers

SILICONE, LATEX AND OTHERS

4D Model Shop
www.modelshop.co.uk
Tel: +44 (0)20 7253 1996
Various liquid rubbers

Alec Tiranti Ltd
www.tiranti.co.uk
Tel: +44 (0)845 123 2100
Silicone and latex

Canonbury Arts
www.canonburyarts.co.uk
Tel: +44 (0)20 7226 4652
Various liquid rubbers

Four-D Rubber Company
www.fourdrubber.com
Tel: +44 (0)1773 763 134
Ready formed and coloured sheet latex

Glowbug Luminescent Colours
www.capricorn.co.uk
Tel: +44 (0)1353 664974
Colour powders for rubbers

Jacobson Chemicals Ltd
www.jacobsonchemicals.co.uk
Tel: +44 (0)1420 86934
Many types of silicone and polyurethane rubbers

Pentonville Rubber Company
www.pentonvillerubber.co.uk
Tel: +44 (0)20 7837 4582
Cord and sheet, neoprene and other rubbers

Trylon
www.trylon.co.uk
Tel: +44 (0)1933 411724
Silicone and latex

Other Sources:

Fishing Shops – Silcone accessories of various kinds, including tubing.

Diving suppliers or shops – Small quantities of rubber solution glues.

TIP

For suppliers near you, try Googling a material and town and see where it leads you.

plastic suppliers

4-D Model Shop
www.modelshop.co.uk
Tel: +44 (0)20 7264 1288
Resins and sheet plastics

Alec Tiranti Ltd
www.tiranti.co.uk
Tel: +44 (0)845 123 2100/(0)20
7380 0808
Resin supplies

Altec Products Ltd
www.altecweb.com
Tel: +44 (0)845 359 9000
Polypropylene rod and sheet silicone tubing.

Buck and Hickman
www.buckandhickman.com
Tel: +44 (0)2476 306444
Wad punches

Canonbury Arts
www.canonburyarts.co.uk
Tel: +44 (0)20 7226 4652
Bio resin

EMA Model Supplies
www.plastruct.co.uk
Tel: +44 (0)1932 228228
Acrylic balls

Fred Aldous
www.fredaldous.co.uk
Tel: +44 (0)161 236 4224
Polypropylene sheeting in various colours

Gilbert Industrial Plastics Ltd
www.theplasticshop.co.uk
Tel: +44 (0)800 321 3085
Various plastics

Hamar Ltd
www.hamaracrylic.co.uk
Tel: +44 (0)207 739 2907
Acrylic stock

Hindleys
www.hindleys.com
Tel: +44 (0)114 278 7828
Various plastics stock

Kemtex Educational Supplies
www.kemtex.co.uk
Tel: +44 (0)1257 230220
Dyes for plastics

Lesley Strickland Jewellery
www.lesley-strickland.co.uk
Email and ask for cellulose acetate offcuts

Plastic Merchants Ltd
10 Church St, Brighton
Tel: +44 (0)1273 329958
Acrylic sheet and rod and offcuts

Precision Plastic Ball Co. Ltd
www.theppb.co.uk
Tel: +44 (0)1943 831166

Quality Colours London Ltd
Unit 13 Gemini Business Estate,
Landmann Way,

London SE14 5RL
Tel: +44 (0)20 7394 8775
Disperse dye wetting agent and carrier for plastics

Ridgway Optical Supplies Ltd
Tel: +44 (0)1295 678800
Call for information
Cellulose acetate.

Trylon Ltd
www.trylon.co.uk
Tel: +44 (0)1933 411 724
Resin and related supplies

Watford Plastics
www.watfordplastics.com
Tel: +44 (0)1923 721011
Nylon and othe plastic stock

Wessex Resins and Adhesives
www.west-system.co.uk
Tel: +44 (0)1794 521111

wood suppliers

Craft Supplies Ltd
www.craft-supplies.co.uk
Tel: +44 (0)800 146417/(0)1433
622550
*Offcuts of exotic woods, veneers
and related supplies*

Foxell and James
www.foxellandjames.co.uk
Tel: +44 (0)20 7405 0152
Dyes and glues

paper & leather suppliers

Abbey Saddlery and Crafts Ltd
www.abbeysaddlery.co.uk
Tel: +44 (0)1565 650343
Leather dyes, for trade only

Alma Leather
www.almahome.co.uk
Tel: +44 (0)20 7377 0762

Falkiners Papers
www.falkiners.com
Tel: +44 (0)20 7831 1151
Leather and paper

Fibrecrafts
www.fibrecrafts.com
Tel: +44 (0)1483 565800
Papermaking supplies

J, Hewit & Sons Ltd
www.hewit.com
Tel: +44 (0) 131 449 2206
Leather, tools and dyes

Handtools-UK
www.handtools-uk.com
Tel: +44 (0)1306 740433
Leather craft tools

Maiko Dawson
www.maikodawson.com
Tel: +44 (0)20 8766 8766
*Leather offcuts - please email and
ask*

Paperchase
Tottenham Court Road,
London/St Mary's Gate,
Manchester
www.paperchase.co.uk

**RT stamping system from
Taylor Designs**
t.designs@btinternet.com
Tel: +44 (0)7961 104183
*Offers a cutting service for
jewellery trade, one-off or quantity,
in metals or plastic and all the
information on using the RT
stamping system*

**Michael Carpenter RT
Cutting Service**
www.michaelcarpenterjewellery.
co.uk
Tel: +44 (0) 1728 861699
*Will do the steel plate cutting
for you*

textile suppliers

George Weil
www.fibrecrafts.com
Tel: +44 (0)1483 565800
Material and equipment – all sorts

The Handweavers' Studio
29 Haroldstone Road
London E17 7AN
Tel: +44 (0)20 8521 2281
Thread and wool

John Lewis PLC
Oxford Street, London
Dissolvable film, metallic threads

Knitting and Crochet Guild
www.kcgtrading.com
Tel: +44 (0)113 2663651
Soluble cloth/film

MacCulloch and Wallis
www.macculloch-wallis.co.uk
Tel: +44 (0)20 7629 0311
Metallic thread.

Madeira
www.madeira.co.uk
Tel: +44 (0)1765 640 003
Embroidery-soluble cloth/film

Oliver Twists
22 Phoenix Road, Washington,
Tyne and Wear, NE38 0AD
*Special cotton threads for
embroidery*

Texere Yarns
www.texere.co.uk
Tel: +44 (0)1274 722191
Yarns

Whaleys (Bradford) Ltd
www.whaleys-bradford.ltd.uk
Tel: +44 (0)1274 576718
Dissolvable cloth/film

William Hall & Co.
Cheadle Hume
Tel: +44 (0)161 437 3295
Swedish linens

Wingham Wool Work
www.winghamwoolwork.co.uk
Tel: +44 (0)1226 742926
Felt and yarns

dye suppliers for textile & plastic

Kemtex Colours
www.kemtex.co.uk/www.textile
dyes.co.uk
Tel: +44 (0)1257 230220

Quality Colours (London) Ltd
Unit 13, Gemini Business Estate,
Landmann Way,
London SE14 5RL
Tel: +44 (0)20 7394 8775

metal suppliers

Aluminium Leicester
11 Putney Road West, Leicester
LE2 7TD
Tel: +44 (0)116 255 3530
Pre-anodised sheet

Caswell
www.caswelleurope.co.uk/anodise.htm
Small quantities of dye info and anodising kits

Chaperlin and Jacobs Ltd
www.chaperlin.co.uk
Tel: +44 (0)20 8641 6996
Steel wire

Clariant Distribution UK Ltd
www.clariant.co.uk
Tel: +44 (0)113 2584 646
Dyes in industrial quantities

Edwards Metals Ltd
37 Birch Road East,
Wyrley Trading Estate, Witton
Birmingham, B6 7DA
Tel: +44 (0)121 322 2366
Base metals

GSM Industrial Graphics
Witney, Oxfordshire,
OX28 4BZ
Tel: +44 (0)1993 776511
Aluminium

Keraplate Ltd
www.keraplate.co.uk
Tel: +44 (0)1202 622882
Pre-anodised sheet

Mackay and Lynn
www.mackayandlynn.co.uk
Tel: +44 (0)131 448 0865
Patination chemicals.

Ormiston Wire
www.ormiston-wire.co.uk
Tel: +44 (0)20 8569 8020
Metal wires and braid

J. Smith and Sons
www.smithmetal.com
Tel: (0)1767 604706
Most of the metals in this book

Titanium Information Group
www.titaniuminfogroup.co.uk

Vitrum Signum
www.vitrumsignum.com
Tel: +44 (0)20 8524 9546
Enamel supplies

stone suppliers

British Lapidary and Mineral Dealers Association
www.blmda.com
Tel: +44 (0)1282 614615
May be able to help with second-hand stone cutting machines

Geologists Online
www.ukge.co.uk
Tel: +44 (0)1502 725447
Useful information on tools and equipment

Hilton Brothers (Lapidary)
www.hiltonbros.com
Tel: +44 (0)161 477 1151
Stone cutting supplies

Manchester Minerals
www.gemcraft.co.uk
Tel: +44 (0)161 477 0435
Stone cutting supplies

other useful suppliers & organisations

SUPPLIERS

Buck and Ryan
www.buckandryan.co.uk
Tel: +44 (0)845 603 4530
Various tools and machinery

Cookson
www.cooksongold.com
Tel: +44 (0)845 100 1122/+44 (0)121 200 2120
Jewellery supplies

H.S. Walsh
www.hswalsh.com
Tel: +44 (0)20 8778 7061
Jewellery supplies

South Western Industrial Plasters
www.industrialplasters.com
Tel: +44 (0)1380 850616
All sorts of equipment and materials

Tufnol Ltd
www.tufnol.com
Tel: +44 (0)121 356 9351
Press stamping material

ORGANISATIONS

Association of Contemporary Jewellery
findings@acj.org.uk

SHORT JEWELLERY COURSES AT:
West Dean College
West Dean, Sussex
www.westdean.org

Birmingham School of Jewellery
Vittoria St. Birmingham
www.jewellery-innovation.co.uk

London Metropolitan University
Sir John Cass Department
www.londonmet.ac.uk

CRAFTS COUNCIL EXHIBITIONS:
Collect, a contemporary art fair for objects at the V&A Museum in London.
www.craftscouncil.org.uk

Origin, the London Craft Fair
Somerset House, London WC2R 1LA
www.craftscouncil.org.uk

Horniman Museum
Forest Hill, SE23 3PQ
www.horniman.ac.uk

Pitt Rivers Museum
University of Oxford, South Parks Rd, Oxford, OX1 3PP
www.prm.ox.ac.uk

Victoria and Albert Museum
Cromwell Rd, London SW7 2RL
www.vam.ac.uk

bibliography

Ashley, Clifford W., *The Ashley Book of Knots* (1993, London: Faber and Faber) 0 571 09659-X

Codina, Carles, *The New Jewellery: Contemporary materials and techniques* (2005, Lark Books) 1-57990-734-2

Hughes, Richard and Rowe, Michael, *The Colouring, Bronzing and Patination of Metal* (1986, Crafts Council) 0 903798 60 3

Lefteri, Chris, *Plastics: Materials for inspirational design* (2001, Rotovision) 2-88046-548-6

McCreight, Tim, *Hot and Cold Connections* (2007, London: A&C Black) 978-0-7136-8758-3

McGrath, Jinks, *The Encyclopedia of Jewellery-making Techniques* 0 7472 7679-X

Olver, Elizabeth, *The Art of Jewellery Design* (2002, London: A&C Black) 1-58180-212-9

Stöfer, Hans, *Wire Jewellery* (2006, London: A&C Black) 0-7136-6634-X

Untracht, Oppi, *Jewelry Concepts and Technology* (1982, Doubleday) 0 385 04185-3

index